RELATIVISM AND RELIGION

Relativism and Religion

Edited by

Charles M. Lewis
Professor of Philosophy
Wake Forest University
Winston-Salem, North Carolina

St. Martin's Press　　　New York

St. Martin's Press, Scholarly and Reference Division,
175 Fifth Avenue, New York, N.Y. 10010

First published in the United States of America in 1995

Printed in Great Britain

ISBN 0–312–12392–2

Library of Congress Cataloging-in-Publication Data
Relativism and religion / edited by Charles M. Lewis.
p. cm.
Essays presented at the ninth James Montgomery Hester seminar.
Includes bibliographical references and index.
ISBN 0–312–12392–2
1. Knowledge, Theory of (Religion) 2. Relativity. I. Lewis, Charles M., 1941– .
BL51.R343 1995
200′ .1—dc20   94–43978
                                                                      CIP

Contents

Notes on the Contributors

Martin Hollis is Professor of Philosophy at the University of East Anglia, Norwich. He was editor of *Ratio* from 1980 through 1988 and has been a Fellow of the British Academy since 1990. Among his books are *Rational Economic Man*, *Rationality and Relativism*, and *The Cunning of Reason*.

Ian Jarvie is Professor of Philosophy at York University, Toronto. He is managing editor of *Philosophy of the Social Sciences* and a fellow of the Royal Society of Canada. His books include *The Revolution in Anthropology*, *Concepts and Society*, and *Thinking about Society: Theory and Practice*.

D. Z. Phillips is Professor of Philosophy at the University College of Swansea and Danforth Professor of the Philosophy of Religion, Claremont Graduate School. Among his books are *The Concept of Prayer*, *Religion Without Explanation*, and *Faith after Foundationalism*.

Philip L. Quinn is John A. O'Brien Professor of Philosophy, University of Notre Dame. He is the author of *Divine Commands and Moral Requirements* and numerous articles and reviews.

Nicholas Wolterstorff is Professor of Philosophical Theology at Yale Divinity School and Adjunct Professor in the Department of Philosophy. He has been appointed Gifford Lecturer for 1994/5. Among his books are *Reason within the Bounds of Religion*, *On Universals*, and *Works and Worlds of Art*.

Introduction

The following papers provide a revealing look at the many faces of relativism as they make their appearance in contemporary philosophy of religion. Their implications for the epistemology of religious belief are examined from several different philosophical perspectives and, in the concluding section, the contributors offer assessments of the papers and the discussions they provoked during the Hester Seminar.

Drawing upon the revolutionary ideas in the work of the later Wittgenstein, D. Z. Phillips attempts to derail traditional approaches to questions about the epistemic status of religious belief claims by rejecting the assumption that "God" in such claims is a name referring to something, to some object or matter of fact. He is convinced that the deep grammar of theistic discourse precludes taking "God" as the *name* of anything. The evidence of objectifying language in sacred texts and traditions notwithstanding, he nevertheless argues that God is not an object in the way anything that is named must be. There is, he thinks, a profound difference between the way two people can be said to speak of the same object, say a person or a planet, and the way two people speak of the same God: "What determines whether [they] are talking of the same God is the spiritual content in what they say." And the spiritual content is determined by the context or practice of religious belief. It is what he calls a confused realist epistemology that supposes one can tell what it means to speak of God as though that were something given apart from the particular religious context within which such language has its life. An implication of this point would be that traditional apologetics, drawing upon metaphysical conceptions of God, is without application.

The question may now arise as to whether Phillips's own position is not, in effect, one of the forms of relativism that has taken root in our century. But a relativist, according to Phillips, would say that should religious practice "die out" so would God be dead. Such is the relativistic conception of the relation between God and belief in God. Phillips' believer, however, would counter this historicizing prospect with the conviction that such a hypothetical could only mean "the world had turned its back on God." This is to note that in religious practice one cannot say that God has died, whatever the case may be concerning the existence or nonexistence of belief in God. To talk about God is not to talk about a matter of fact, but to say that is not to deny the reality of God. Yet what it means to talk about the reality of God is not something that can be determined apart from an examination of its *religious* use. And the language of religious practice shows that such a reality is "spiritual," that what one is talking about is not clarified by thinking of it as a fact or an object any more than "pain" is clarified by thinking of it as referring to a "sort of 'something'." In its religious sense the reality of God is not that of anything that may die or cease to exist.

The point here is that what these words mean cannot be determined independently of the particular contexts in which they are used. The contexts Phillips has in mind are those in which words have their ordinary, as opposed to some artificial or metaphysical, use. The latter use is a case of what Wittgenstein called "subliming" the logic of language. Only in the "living contexts" of belief and practice can one find the (proper) sense of words or expressions. Only there do they have their application. So a relativistic concept of God as an internal or context-dependent object of belief is an artificial conception of God that has lost touch with the original contexts wherein it has its religious life and meaning.

For Martin Hollis, on the other hand, Phillips does not thereby avoid relativism. His is, indeed, a radical relativism that is no less than an affront to the traditional believer, for whom belief in God is belief in a matter of objective fact and may thus be supported by appeal to matters of fact that do not depend upon religious contexts. Where the grounds for belief can be only other beliefs in a "web of beliefs," theoretical posits are supposed to replace objective facts. But since God is supposed to be an objective fact, the relativism that would make God a context-dependent posit is precluded.

Hollis argues, more fully in previous papers, that the very ability to identify differences among beliefs from various contexts presupposes that we have common knowledge. He calls this knowledge "a set of common beliefs which make common sense of a common world." Without such common "bridgehead" beliefs, different cultures would be unable to understand each other at all and the translation of languages would be impossible. But since cross-cultural understanding and translation are manifestly possible, certain non-relative, common beliefs are necessary *a priori*. The "bridgehead" beliefs are (or include?) "simple perceptual judgments" about what have been called "middle-sized ... enduring solid objects," including human beings.

But having made this case against a relativism that would leave us with no common objects, Hollis thinks, nevertheless, that the matter is otherwise when it comes to beliefs about things such as spirits or the particles of scientific theories. Where such things seem to be so manifestly internal to particular theories or conceptual schemes, one is hard pressed to gainsay the relativistic claim that they are the posits of those theories or schemes. Hollis acknowledges that the "convinced believer" does not think his God (or gods, etc.) is solely a matter of his – or anyone's – beliefs, nor, for that matter, does the naturalist think that way about his particles. But while Hollis rejects the sort of relativism that undermines the truth-seeking of both naturalism and hermeneutics, he hedges his bets as to whether religious claims are, in fact, true. He has in mind here truths about the "unseen world," which, as he sees it, is "a reading of spiritual truths about this world."

Though Hollis seems to think this is a minority version of a religious, as opposed to a naturalistic, interpretation of religion, it is clear enough that his version does not ring true for Philip Quinn. Its "reductionistic flavor," he says, seems too much like Feuerbachian projection theories of religion. Rather than pressing an analogy between theoretical particles and God, Quinn follows William Alston in pressing an analogy between perceiving sensory objects and the religious or mystical experience of God. Though some religious beliefs (e.g. in divine simplicity or eternity) are manifestly "secondary" and thus relative to particular conceptual schemes, others are perceptual beliefs of a certain kind and thus not "threatened by arguments for semantic relativism in the domain of secondary theory." As for epistemic relativism in the domain of religious belief, Quinn is resigned to that. There are, he thinks, no context-independent criteria of what counts as being justified or rational. It is the semantic or metaphysical kind of relativism that he rejects.

Quinn's critique of Joseph Runzo's case for religious relativism examines a kind of semantic relativism about truth. Runzo's case is based upon what he calls "conceptual relativism," according to which "truth is relative in the strong sense of there being mutually incompatible, yet individually adequate, sets of conceptual-schema-relative truths." Runzo thinks the application of this relativism to religious claims makes an advance upon religious pluralism such as that of John Hick. He agrees that the conceptual schemes of the world's religions are multiple representations of the same "noumenal ultimate," but he argues that these schemes determine different world orders corresponding to which are mutually incompatible sets of truth claims. So, then, it is allowable that what is vital or distinctive in more than one of the great religious traditions is true – i.e. relative to the respective schemes and their world orders.

The religious ultimate – or "phenomenal" divine reality – of these world orders has been conceived in some religions as personal and in others as impersonal. But what would it mean to say that both conceptions are true? Runzo's relativism seems to be saying only that relative to one conceptual scheme the phenomenal ultimate is personal and relative to another it is impersonal. In which case his relativizing of *truth* is no more than, as Quinn says, a misleading *façon de parler*. The two claims, being about different phenomenal ultimates, are not incompatible. It is true, literally and nonrelatively, that in one kind of schema the phenomenal ultimate is personal and in another impersonal. Putting the matter in terms of the one and only "noumenal" ultimate makes no difference. For the claim that the noumenal ultimate manifests itself in one kind of schema as personal and in another as impersonal amounts to no more than the claim that the noumenal ultimate stands in one relation to one kind of conceptual scheme and in another relation to the other kind. And there is nothing in this that would make Runzo's relativism anything more or other than a version of religious pluralism. Even reference, as in Hick's case, is secured by the noumenal ultimate. The relativizing of truth here is simply a superfluous move, reducible to nonrelative truth about different relations. Thus Quinn finds no foothold in this philosophy of religion for semantic relativism.

Whereas Quinn and Hollis find limited areas in which relativism reigns, Ian Jarvie takes relativism in any form whatever to be ill-conceived. Following Karl Popper and W. W. Bartley, he traces the source of this misconception to the assumption that the adjudication of claims requires the justification of claims and that justification is based, ultimately, upon what is known without qualification, upon what is truly foundational. But the only way to secure the alleged foundation so that it requires no further justification is by the arbitrary declaration that it is self-justifying. There is no other recourse for those who rely upon rational intuition, sense data, authoritative texts, or whatever else that may be taken as ultimate. Relativism is what is left when the foundation turns out to be only one among other acknowledged bases of justification.

In particular Jarvie notes the "fideistic" kind of relativism, in which one secures one's own foundation or "form of life" as being simply ultimate for oneself and one's society. Certain followers, at least, of the later Wittgenstein are thus located in this cul-de-sac. But contrary to their presumption of security, what is taken to be self-justifying is nevertheless fair game for criticism – not, however, the traditional kind of criticism that presumes a yet deeper security in some universal foundation beneath all forms of life. That is to say, for Jarvie's "non-justificationist" the proper way to adjudicate among competing claims – whether axiological (as the "value" claims of morality and religion) or scientific – is to see how "criticizable they are and how well criticized they have been." Since nothing is beyond criticism, not even the laws of logic, there is no final security, only more or less progress in the critique of ideas. So not even the assessment of what counts as progress is somehow exceptional or beyond controversy. Nevertheless, where one finds progress there one finds the answer to relativism.

It seems clear that Jarvie's paradigm of progress is modern natural science. Here, above all, criticism is invited (presumably so long as only "scientific" criteria are applied) and only the theories that have so far survived criticism are taken seriously. It is, though, less clear how one is to understand progress when applied to his axiological domain. In one place he seems to be saying that it is progress in natural science that motivates advances in moral values. At least his remarks about eugenics in his response to Hollis suggest that we have the progress of science to thank for exposing its errors. Hence "fideistic dogmatisms" like Aryan science can be progressive only in a "strictly circumscribed sense." If Jarvie's point about eugenics is taken as an example of moral as well as scientific progress, his position would have much in common with E. O. Wilson's attempt to link the two domains. Presumably the same would be said of those values deemed religious and the outcome for both religion and morality would be a continual erosion of values, even long-cherished ones, that are found to be incompatible with scientific progress. A relativist, on the other hand, being bound by what is given in his extant social system (unless a purely arbitrary appeal is made to some other) can only stand in the way of real progress here. Such progress for Jarvie is identifiable with liberalism, as opposed to conservative "impotence and appeasement."

Although he does not treat relativism as it pertains to knowledge claims generally or to religious claims in particular, Nicholas Wolterstorff sees in the plurality of interpretations and uses of canonical texts within a religion something like the larger issue. And rather than discussing this plurality as it pertains to relativism, he examines Hans Frei's attempt to confront the many different interpretations that have characterized Christian thinking for the past three hundred years. Without a proper appreciation of the "realistic narrative character of the literal sense of the text," the Gospels are subject to whatever interpretations seem to follow upon what is already taken to be true and edifying. Using ideas shared with the Anglo-American New Criticism, Frei takes the very givenness of the Gospels and their literal sense to be the unifying basis for the Christian community's reading of its central texts. The practice of interpreting these texts, then, should be distinguished from their appropriation by the community via judgments about their truth and utility. Neither their truth nor their use to the community should intrude upon the practice of interpreting their literal sense in a literary way. Wolterstorff notes, however, that Frei does require a closer connection than this point would suggest, since he upholds the realistic narrative on account of its value to the community. This value would come from joining the interpretation of the literal sense as realistic narrative to its appropriation by transforming it into actual history at the critical point of Jesus' identity. But the interpretation itself must be secured against questions about whether the texts are fiction or history or to what extent they are one or the other, etc. Whatever one might think about any of this, Wolterstorff argues that even the interpretation itself of works of fiction should notice where assertions, for example, are being made, and thus bring into play questions about truth and utility. What the text says has illocutionary force as well as what Frei assumes is its sense *qua* propositional content.

The essays that follow were read and discussed at the ninth James Montgomery Hester Seminar, held at Wake Forest University, March 20 and 21, 1992. This seminar is endowed by a generous gift from James Montgomery Hester, a 1917 graduate of Wake Forest, in honor of Professor A. C. Reid, beloved teacher and chairman of the Department of Philosophy for many years.

1

Where are the Gods Now?

D. Z. Phillips

I

In *Belief, Changes and Forms of Life* I said: "It is a misunderstanding to speak of religion as a form of life. What can be said is that it is impossible to imagine a religion without imagining it *in* a form of life. What happens to a religion in a form of life cannot be laid down in advance. It is a matter of its fate in a complex network of influences and counter-influences."[1]

To many philosophers of religion, admitting that religion is subject to the play of circumstances has unacceptable consequences. For them, it implies that the eternal is at the mercy of the temporal: that the unchanging reality of God has been made subject to that which comes to be and passes away. Philosophers who are disposed to react in this way will hardly be reassured by what I went on to say about three futile comforting pictures which seek to avoid the challenge of cultural change to religion.

I called the first comforting picture *religious individualism*.[2] According to this picture, a believer has a direct relationship with his Saviour in his heart. This secret place, it is claimed, is immune to secular challenges and changes in the surrounding culture. I argued that this notion of immunity is confused. If the culture declines, one cannot guarantee that, in time, there will not also be a decline in the thoughts in men's hearts.

I called the second comforting picture *religious rationalism*:[3] the view that the validity of formal proofs of the existence of God transcends all cultural change. I argued: "So far from it being the formal proofs which give a rational foundation to the beliefs of the faithful, it was the lives of the faithful which breathed into the formal proofs whatever life they had."[4]

I called the third comforting picture *religious accommodation*:[5] the view that, by taking new forms, Christianity can always accommo-

1

date any cultural change. I argued that one cannot say, in general, that all forms of accommodation constitute religious progress. Some may constitute decadence and decline. Faced by the possibilities of cultural change, philosophy cannot indulge in *a priori* optimism or *a priori* pessimism.

I mention these arguments here, not to rehearse them, but to consider a further likely reaction to them. It will be argued that even if the direst cultural changes are imagined, they are simply irrelevant as far as the reality of God is concerned. All my arguments establish, it will be said, is the obvious fact that religion may be more or less healthy in a culture at any given time. But, the counter-argument runs, this has nothing to do with God's reality, since whether God exists does not depend on such cultural realities. The believer holds that God exists no matter what we care to say or think. Religious attitudes wax or wane, but God's existence is an unchanging, objective fact.

In this essay, I want to explore the appeal of these philosophical reactions. They seem to have such an obvious justification: no one would believe in God unless he believed that God exists. In some circumstances that remark might be entirely unexceptional. In philosophy, on the other hand, it may lull us into accepting a confused realist epistemology. We think that the sense of "believing that God exists" is simply "given," without reference to the contexts within which such belief has its meaning. This is a case of what Wittgenstein called "subliming the logic of our language." We abstract a phrase such as "it is the case that" from all its diverse applications and assume that *its* name is the same, whether we are talking of the chair in the next room, my bank balance, someone's love for me, the genuineness of an expression, or the existence of God. I do not want to repeat my arguments against religion of this kind.[6] Rather, I want to explore further how these philosophical reactions have a particular bearing on issues concerning religion and relativism.

II

On entering large art museums or institutes, I have often been annoyed to discover the long corridors one has to traverse in order to arrive at their collection of impressionist paintings. I have to pass the innumerable exhibits in the Egyptian section, where, to me in my ignorance, one mummy looks much like another. But on one occasion, hurrying along as usual, I was suddenly struck by the fact that I was hurrying past the gods! Rows upon rows of them: gods of the Upper Nile and gods of the Lower Nile.

So is this where the gods end up? A case of Who Was Who among the gods, the cards signifying how long it has been since anyone worshipped them? The religions and their gods have become no more than museum relics: anthropological stories I can hear as long as I have the money to insert for the commentary.

Again, a reaction to these fears can be anticipated: "Your fears are groundless. You are talking about gods, not about God. Of course, gods can end up as museum exhibits, but God never could. The God with whom there is no variableness or shadow of turning cannot share such a fate. The Lord of Creation is not an artist's arte-fact." And if the person who so reacts has taken a course or two in philosophy, he may well add: "The gods you mention are relative to a culture whose products they were. God transcends all cultures. His reality is absolute, not relative."

This reaction has more than one aspect. Some aspects are clearly confused. For example, there is the implication that unlike the relics of Egyptian religion, relics of Christianity could not be found in museums. But after the corridors of pre-Christian art come corri-dors of Christian art. Moreover I see, not simply early relics, but paintings no longer in their religious settings, vestments no longer worn, altars before which no one kneels, and crucifixes not contem-plated in worship. Could not that be the ultimate fate of *all* vest-ments, altars and crucifixes?

Within the philosophical reaction we are considering, however, a further response will be made at this point. Even if it is allowed that Christianity could share the fate of Egyptian religion, it will be said that this misses the essential issue of God's reality with which one must begin. The difference between God and the gods, accord-ing to this view, may be put like this: if we regard all the artistic items in the museums as names, then only in the case of the Judeo-Christian religion does the name have a bearer. The names of gods have no bearer. The objective reality of God does not depend on the fate of names: it depends on the existence of the bearer of the name. In the case of divine names, there is only one bearer of a name. That is why the existence of God transcends the claims of relativism. Once this is recognized, it is argued, we can appreciate two functions fulfilled by the bearer of the divine name. First, it refers to the transcendent cause which sustains Christianity and which sees to it that Christianity does not share the fate of dead religions. Second, the existence of the bearer of the divine name is the justification of the believer's faith.

The reference to God as a metaphysical cause which sees to it that Christianity is sustained, does violence to the grammar of "divine activity." To see God's hand in history is not to see God as externally related to that history. To see God in victory or defeat is not to say that by some quasi-causal operation God brought about the victory or defeat. It is to meet victory or defeat in God. No doubt someone in the grip of his emotivist past will say that this reduces religion to an attitude to the facts: the victory or defeat are the facts, religion is one attitude among many one can take to them. But what is an attitude? Wittgenstein spoke of our response to others as human beings as "an attitude towards a soul." What are the facts in this case? Are the facts supposed to be the biological facts about human beings, while our responses to human beings are the attitudinal appendages? Surely not. Take away our characteristic responses to others and you take away our sense of the human at the same time. Seeing God in the facts makes a substantive difference to what the facts are. It may mean being able to conquer without demoralizing or dehumanizing the vanquished. It may mean being able to receive grace in defeat without feeling bought. This would be involved in seeing victor and vanquished as God's children, and it makes a real difference.

Once we give up the confusing picture of God as an external, causal power who brings about victory or defeat, we give up, at the same time, the assumption that God can see to it that Christianity does not pass out of existence. Simone Weil says that no event is a favor on God's part. That includes the continuation of Christianity. To see grace as God's only favor is to see that Christianity's survival is not underwritten or guaranteed by a metaphysical notion of divine causality.

The second function ascribed to the bearer of the divine name is to act as the metaphysical justification of the believer's faith. The existence of the only bearer of a divine name shows why all other religious beliefs are relative. While it is fitting to call those beliefs relative, belief in the true religion is fittingly called objective. This is another instance of subliming the logic of our language. It may be compared with Wittgenstein's remarks about the role of the King in chess. The role gets its name from the game. It adds nothing to say "And it is fitting that it should be so," as though one were appealing to some further external justification of the game. A believer may wonder at the survival of Christianity. He may call it a gift of grace. He may even say it is fitting that it should be so. But that is an expression of thanksgiving, not the invoking of an external, metaphysical underpinning for faith. In this context, the expression "it is fitting" is idle outside faith; it does no work. An appeal to "religious realities" does not underwrite religious practice, since it is only in terms of such practice that talk of religious realities makes sense.

It is no surprise to find that the two functions ascribed to the bearer of the divine name are confused, since "God" is not a name. Hence it is confused to look for the bearer of the name. In this picture, the bearer of the name is thought of as some kind of object which the word "God" stands for. The kind of talk which is influencing us is that in which we refer to the same person, the same church, the same planet, etc. But when we look at how we would establish identities in these contexts, we see that nothing of this kind enters into considerations as to whether two people worship *the same God*.

We miss the grammatical differences involved if we say that, in the religious case, we are ready to take the existence of the bearer of the divine name on trust. The confusion is deepened if we say that, while the bearers of the names of physical objects are available to us, the bearer of the divine name, being transcendent, is not. Further confusion is created if we say that faith in the absent bearer will be justified eschatologically, when we shall find that there is only one true God, a discovery which answers all relativistic arguments.

Such confused talk keeps in place a grammar which simply does not apply to "God." We are not confronted by what is unavailable. On the contrary, our talk of God is as available as any other talk and we are endeavouring to clarify its grammar. What determines whether two people are talking of the same God is the spiritual content in what they say. It is this content which reveals proximities or distances between them. This being so, the confused grammar does violence to this spirituality. That is why Wittgenstein said that even if we imagined events happening of a kind the confused grammar would lead us to expect, they could not fulfill the religious purposes these "events" were supposed to have. We can illustrate this in terms of three examples: the Last Judgment, eternal life and finding God.

If we think of the Last Judgment as the name of a future event, in the sense that it would be a judgment after the-last-but-one, little sense can be made of it as the judgment of eternity it is supposed to be. The judgment is posed as a future threat which is supposed to modify my present conduct. The trouble is that this kind of modification has little to do with morality or religion. It seems to be a case of self-interest transcendentalized. Threatened by it, Socrates would reply as he did to Polus in the *Gorgias*: "You are trying to frighten me with bogeys." To a threat of hell, so conceived, Don Giovanni was right to say "No!" So even if a last judgment of this kind occurred, it would have no religious significance. Contrast this with Simone Weil's remark that one of the deepest conceptions of hell is thinking one is in paradise when one is not.

Part of the confusion involved is that of turning an eternal judgment into a temporal one. We are not told the time of the Last Judgment when we are informed that it is "at the end of time." Eternity is not a matter of duration. If we think of eternal life as the name of continued existence after death, then this "temporal immortality," as Wittgenstein calls it, could not fulfill any religious purpose. Wittgenstein asks why this continued life should be any less puzzling than his present one.

In this continued existence, we are supposed to find God, locate the bearer of the name "God" and, by so doing, resolve all the questions of relativism by establishing the objectivity of religious belief. But, once again, such a view serves no religious purpose, since it does violence to what "finding God" means. To speak of "finding God" or "coming to God" is to speak of the emergence of spiritual awareness. The locating of the bearer of the name we are offered, by contrast, is simply the location of another object which we may or may not be able to explain. In neither event, as John Wisdom pointed out, would this amount to coming to God. A nice theological joke about Paul Tillich reaching heaven illustrates the point well. Tillich found himself confronted by an old man who said to him. "Professor Tillich, I'm God." "But you're an old man!" cried Tillich in amazement. "True," answered the old man. "A discrete individual; an object among objects," exclaimed Tillich. "Quite so," said the old man. "In that case," Tillich replied, "take me to your leader!"

III

Locating the bearer of the divine name is thought to have a special role in resolving questions concerning moral relativity. Even if we put aside the grammatical confusions involved in treating "God" as a name, it is difficult to see how this resolution of the questions is supposed to be achieved.

The issues concerning relativity and morality may be expressed as follows.[7] I have within me selfish and altruistic tendencies. The former may be said to be the more natural in their origin, whereas the latter are the result of parental instruction. It is admitted that we cannot show, by utilitarian considerations, or by appeal to human good and harm, why altruism should be preferred to selfishness. Altruism and selfishness cannot be cashed into a common coinage or be subjected to a common measure by means of which the superiority of one or the other can be demonstrated. To think otherwise is to be confused. Yet, it is argued, being free of this confusion does not lay to rest the challenge of relativism. On the contrary, the challenge is strengthened, for if there is no common measure by which altruism and selfishness can be assessed, how is one to choose between them? In logic, one attitude has no more hold on me than the other.

No satisfactory answer can be given to this question, it is said, unless we invoke the existence of God. If I believe in the existence of God, and that it is his will that I should be altruistic, I am no longer confronted simply by a clash of attitudes or perspectives. One of these perspectives corresponds to the will of the Lord of the Universe. Altruism is not simply one perspective among many. It is the will of God. If my worry was about the relativity of perspectives, establishing that God exists gets rid of *that* worry. The difficulty, however, is in seeing how this claim is justified.

Let us make the challenge more difficult by putting aside the suggestion that altruism is no more than conformity to parental teaching. After all, the view does not bear examination. We can distinguish between a conforming altruism and a genuine regard for the virtue. The latter cannot be reduced to the former. Neither does the fact that my parents instructed me in the exercise of this virtue make its moral importance suspect. To think otherwise is to commit the genetic fallacy. My thinking altruism is important *now* is not a matter of invoking parental authority. In elucidating the importance it has, I talk about altruism, not about my parents.

What are the consequences of saying that altruism and selfishness have an equal logical status? As we have seen, what saying this amounts to is that there is no common measure between them by means of which it can be shown why I should be altruistic.

But does it have the perplexing consequence that I do not know how to choose between them? What is this state of perplexity supposed to be?

If I am selfish, I shall regard altruistic duties as interferences and inconveniences to be avoided or negotiated if possible. If I acknowledge the worth of altruism, I already know that I should not be selfish. There will be situations where I waver between them: I may be tempted to be selfish or find my selfishness surprisingly succumbing in a situation where altruism is called for. These situations of tension are found in the commonplace and in extreme cases. Hardy's Jude finds all his high-minded plans for his future swept aside by the condescension of a county girl to go for a walk with him in her Sunday frock and ribbons. Benjamin Britten's Claggart, confronted by the innocence of Billy Budd, finds that the order of his inner hell has been challenged; a light shone in the darkness, and the darkness comprehended it and trembled. Outside these contexts of genuine tension, what does the question "Which shall I choose?" amount to? It seems to be an artificial question. Of course, the question may be raised in philosophy. It may be thought that the absence of a common measure by which altruism and selfishness can be assessed does lead to arbitrariness and relativism. But then this philosophical confusion is dispelled in the way already indicated: by showing that non-arbitrariness does not depend on the existence of a common measure.

What the argument offers as the solution to moral relativity, however, is not such a common measure but the existence of God. His existence *is* supposed to give me an external justification for being altruistic rather than selfish. But suppose I am a selfish person and find out that the demands of altruism actually have a lawgiver? Why should this make me change my mind? The lawgiver's existence may simply be an additional object of my annoyance. But does it not make a difference if the author is Lord of the Universe? Maybe, but what kind of difference? Suppose I recognize that, since I am up against the Lord of the Universe, my selfish plans are necessarily frustrated, that the divine plan will not allow them to come to fruition. It may then be argued that continued selfishness would be irrational. But if I conform to God's will for these reasons, the result will not be altruism but the kind of servility with which it can be contrasted.

Further difficulties occur once we go beyond a simple contrast between altruism, a good, and selfishness, an evil. We go beyond this contrast once we recognize different moral perspectives, some of which are anti-religious in character. Among the latter are those which deny God's existence. The deniers take themselves to be saying that a certain kind of object does not, indeed, cannot exist. Confronted by an object of that kind, their denials would have to be abandoned. God does exist after all! But for the opponent of religion this makes matters even worse. Locating the bearer of the divine name does not weaken his opposition to religion; it strengthens it.

For the two reasons we have noted, locating the bearer of the divine name will not answer problems of moral relativity. In the case of the relativism said to hold between morality and immorality, acknowledging the existence of a God who can necessarily frustrate one's selfish desires cannot effect the kind of practice of altruism morality requires. All it brings about is a conformity to altruism, which is no more than selfishness operating under constraints. Thus, invoking God's existence does not provide the required reason by reference to which altruism is to be preferred to selfishness. In the case of the relativity said to hold between different moral perspectives, locating God cannot resolve the disagreement between them, since how the being located is viewed will itself depend on the moral perspective from which it is viewed. In the first context, then , locating God does not guarantee the appropriation of a genuine virtue. In the second context, locating God cannot guarantee that the God located will be thought of as virtuous at all. The relativity said to exist between morality and immorality, and between different moral perspectives, remains.

These difficulties could be overcome if it could be argued that God is good in himself, meaning by this that, once God is seen to exist, that very fact guarantees the appropriate response. Thus, it would have to be argued that a selfish person, coming into God's presence, would immediately forsake his selfish ways. It would also have to be argued that any person who embraced an anti-religious moral perspective would, of necessity, on entering God's presence, abandon that perspective immediately. In both cases the mere presence of God, the fact of his existence, of itself necessarily generates the proper response.

The argument simply does not work. The role assigned to God in it is akin to the role Moore's non-natural property of goodness is supposed to play in his *Principia Ethica*. Moore argued that from the recognition of this property, it follows that it would and should be desired. The property is good in itself. To recognize the property is at the same time to recognize that it is good that it should exist. John Anderson pointed out that this claim conflates the use of "good" as a property and its use as a relation. He accused Moore of the fallacy of relativism in this sense. Anderson points out that a claim that something ought to be done is relative to a context in which people have a regard for certain considerations.

> In any usage, to say that an action is right is to say that it 'is to be done', and this raises the question *on what consideration* it is to be done. Now ... this consideration may be a particular movement, ie, it is the movement that 'calls for' the action – but this is really to say no more than that the action does (or would, if performed) further the movement. Or it may be said more generally that the rightness of the action is its furthering *something* – something that can be agreed upon by the people who use the word 'right' – but that, if no such thing were agreed upon or assumed to be agreed upon, the word would never be used.[8]

Moore had argued that the property "good" was, like yellow, unanalyzable. Thus there was no wider context beyond these "simples" in which the claim that it is good that this property should exist can be elucidated. Anderson brings out the logical difficulties in such a view:

> We say 'This is red' or 'This is spherical': but it would be non-sense to say 'It is red that this, and this alone should exist' or 'It is spherical that this, and this alone should exist'. The assertions, 'This is good' and 'It is good that this should exist', are intelligible (and compatible) *only* if we take a relational view of goodness – only if they have some such meaning as 'This is demanded (or commanded)' and 'It is demanded (or commanded) that this should exist'. If, on the other hand, we regard good as a quality, as a characteristic of a thing without further reference, then 'It is good that this should exist' has no meaning.[9]

IV

It is time to take stock of where our arguments have led us. In the first section of the essay I argued that there is no good reason for saying that Christianity is not subject to cultural change. Three comforting pictures, religious individualism, religious rationalism and religious accommodation, sought to obscure that fact. Once admitted, however,it raises fears of relativism, that the reality of Christianity is relative to the culture of which it is the product. If that culture declines, so will Christianity, and it may well end, like other dead religions, as no more than a collection of artistic and anthropological exhibits in a museum.

In the second part of the essay, I considered the argument that states that the reality of God is independent of cultural contingencies. This amounted to saying that the difference between Christianity and the gods of other religions is that only in the Judeo-Christian tradition does the divine name have a bearer. The location of the bearer of the name is the location of the metaphysical cause which sustains Christianity and which affords a rational justification of religious belief. The fundamental objection to this is that "God" is not a name and that therefore searching for the bearer of the name is futile. Thus, even if bearers were envisaged for the names of divine events or for the name "God," they would not fulfill the religious purposes they were meant to serve. I illustrated this by reference to the notions of the Last Judgment, eternal life, and discovering God.

In the third part of the essay, I examined the view that locating the bearer of the divine name resolves the problems arising from moral relativism. I argued that such a location does not resolve the relativity thought to arise from the clash between morality and immorality and the clash between rival moral perspectives.

Given the arguments in the three sections of the essay, we have to conclude that certain attempts to meet the challenge of relativism in the name of religion all fail. That being so, the challenge of relativism seems all the stronger. This challenge can be brought out if we consider wider difficulties concerning Moore's characterization of "good" as an indefinable property. These difficulties have to do with concept-formation. For Moore, the meanings of unanalyzable simples are grayed simply by being confronted by the property in question. He gave "yellow" as an example. But we do not learn what "yellow" means simply by being confronted, say, by a yellow patch. The patch, of itself, does not communicate its meaning. We cannot learn what "yellow" means without at the same time learning what is not yellow. We learn to pick out differences between colors. That possibility depends on the agreement which shows itself in the reactions of human beings. We do not first recognize colors and then react to them. Rather, it is in the context of our shared reactions that distinctions between different colors have their sense. Moore's conception of "simples" which convey their sense without any mediation is, therefore, radically confused.

The same general epistemological point can be made about religious reactions and their role in concept-formation in religion. But there is one important difference: our religious reactions do not exhibit the same general agreement found in our color-reactions. Nevertheless, without some shared religious reactions, no sense could be made of religious disputes concerning what is and what is not of God. Without the Messianic tradition no sense can be made of the disagreements over whether Jesus was the Son of God. His mere presence did not guarantee a worshipful response. We do not first determine who Jesus is and subsequently decide to respond in certain ways. Rather, it is only in the context of our responses that the acknowledgment or denial of who he is makes sense. It may be said, more generally, that we do not first recognize God and subsequently decide to respond in certain ways. Neither is "God" a "simple" which guarantees the response to itself. It was, after all, in heaven that the angels rebelled. It is only in the context of our responses that sense can be made of the reality of God. Our responses show the character of the God we worship; it may be said that they reveal his spirit.

That the spirit in worship should reveal the nature of the God worshipped should not be surprising, since God is a Spiritual reality, and worship is said to be the practice of this spirit. "God is Spirit and they who worship him must worship him in spirit and in truth." Some may think that this emphasis on "spirit" reduces theology to anthropology. They will remind us that we speak of "spirit" in other connections too. We speak of the spirit of movement, the spirit of an age, and so on. Yet, when the movement is over and the age has passed, it would be confused to hypostatize their spirit as though it were something which transcended them. A religion may well have a certain spirit, but when it dies, in this context too, one cannot hypostatize the spirit as though it had an independent existence. When a person dies we sometimes say "He's gone. The life in him has departed." Does not a time come when the gods depart, the life goes out of them, leaving their corpses in the museums – the mortal remains of the gods? Feuerbach was right, to be serious; theology must be anthropology.

The price of this awareness is the admission that religion is relative to the cultural context in which it flourishes and that God has no existence independent of it. So the argument runs.

These conclusions will be invoked by the realist as evidence of the unsatisfactoriness of the analysis I have presented. The reality of God, he argues, is clearly independent of cultural change: "Before the mountains were brought forth, or ever thou hadst formed the earth, from everlasting to everlasting, thou art God." When the earth was dark and void and without form, God's spirit is said to have moved on the face of the waters.

The trouble with this argument is that it makes use of religious expressions without exploring their grammar. We have already seen that "God," unlike "mountain," is not the name of an object. There is a corresponding difference in the grammar of saying that mountains and God existed before men. The sense of what we say about mountains, in this respect, is bound up with the ways in which we talk of physical objects. On the other hand, it makes no sense to talk of banking as existing before man, since banking is a social institution.

But what of the existence of God? God is said to exist before man. But the sense of saying so depends on how we think and talk of God. We may make a comparison with how we talk of beauty. Different cultures have different conceptions of beauty. Some African tribes have no conception of walking for pleasure. While they may regard artifacts as magnificent, waterfalls and mountains are never called beautiful; they are simply there. Does it follow from such a variety that nothing can be said about the beauty of the world prior to the existence of human beings? Not at all. Given certain ways of talking about beauty, it makes sense to wonder that a beautiful valley existed for so long before anyone saw it. Some philosophers would want to analyze this possibility in terms of a counter-factual conditional. All we mean by calling the valley beautiful in such circumstances, they suggest, is that if the valley had been seen at the time, it would have been called beautiful. That analysis will not do. It omits the object of the wonder. Wondering at unseen beauty becomes a matter of how we would react had it been seen. Simone Weil says that a forest is at its most beautiful when there is no one looking at it. A believer may say that only God was looking at it. The counter-factual analysis fails to capture the importance of these remarks. To think otherwise is like thinking that the truth of those advertisements which proclaim the beauty of solitary beaches is realized when thousands of holiday-makers turn up to verify it!

As with the beauty of an unobserved forest, so in the case of God's spirit moving on the face of the waters a religious person may speak of God's contemplation of himself. God, like beauty, has no biography. Only in manic philosophical discussions would anyone think it makes sense to speak of the duration or speed of the spirit's movement! Nevertheless, if people came to think in this way, a certain spiritual vocabulary would be lost to us. The relativist would say that God dies with the demise of this way of thinking. No such conclusion follows, since the language of faith allows the believer to speak of such an eventuality. He would say that the world had turned its back on God.

In speaking of God as Spirit in the way I have done, I am not emphasizing something called the expressive side of religion, at the expense of what some philosophers call its captive or ontological dimension. I am simply elucidating the grammar of our use of "God." Saying God is Spirit is a primary use of the word "God," a use which rules out asking "The spirit of what?" Once this is realized, it follows that what a believer says about religions other than his own, or about different traditions within his own religion, is itself a matter of spiritual discernment. If the same spirit can be found in more than one religion, this constitutes a difficulty for the exclusivist. Coming into contact with religions other than one's own may extend one's conception of the spiritual. Acknowledgment of a spiritual reality takes the form, not of a factual assertion, but of a confession: "Thou art God." The parameters of this confession, though they may be extended from time to time, determine what the believer means by false gods.

Anyone who asks for a determination concerning the true God, without invoking any spiritual considerations, is asking for the impossible. The theoretical question "Apart from any confession of belief, who is the true God?" is a bogus question. Truth in religion is itself a spiritual matter. There is, therefore, an ineradicable personal element in religion.

This brings us back to the early part of the paper. I spoke of myself hurrying past the relics of dead religions in museums. But, to some extent, I am speaking for myself when I say this. I can give "dead religions" a purely descriptive use by saying that I mean religions no longer practiced. But in saying that I hurry past dead gods, I also show where I stand. After all, many hurry past crucifixes as I hurry past the gods of the Nile. But what would the believers of the dead religions say? They could say that I am ignoring divine realities, realities which judge me for my disrespectful haste. Someone may want to ask: "Were you hurrying past divine realities? Just tell me, straightforwardly, 'Yes' or 'No,' without invoking anything spiritual or confessional in your reply." I have yet to come across a form of *that* question which makes sense. In other words, the question "Where are the gods now?" has no theoretical answer.

Notes

1. *Belief, Changes and Forms of Life* (London: Macmillan, 1986), p. 79.
2. Ibid., pp. 84f.
3. Ibid., pp. 90f.
4. Ibid., pp. 91f.
5. Ibid.
6. See "On Really Believing" and "Searle on Language Games and Religion" in my collection, *Wittgenstein and Religion* (London: Macmillan, 1992).
7. I owe this way of expressing the problem to my colleague H. O. Mounce. This is not to say that he would agree exactly with my account of the position.
8. John Anderson. "The Meaning of Good," in *Studies in Empirical Philosophy* (London: Angus and Robertson, 1962), pp. 251–2.
9. Ibid., p. 253.

2

A Prayer for Understanding

Martin Hollis

"Lorde, Thou knowest that I must be very busie this day. If I forget Thee, do not Thou forget me." Sir Jacob Astley, a royalist general in the English Civil War, entered this blunt prayer in his diary just before the Battle of Edgehill in 1642. It is addressed by one officer to another. God, as supreme C.O., will know that there is work to do and that it will be better done if He is out of mind until close of play. Being a no-nonsense sort of chap, He will be expecting Sir Jacob to put up a good show and will not forget him. No doubt similar prayers are being offered by the Cromwellians, no less convinced that they are doing God's work. But even though He might give them credit for sincerity and good soldiering, they are misguided. God is squarely on the King's side.

In taking the prayer so simply, I do not imply that Astley was unreflective, merely that he was busy. He was doubtless aware of deep disputes about the nature of God between Catholics and Protestants or, more abstractly, Aristotelians and Platonists, or, more broadly, Christianity and other religions. But his soldierly view of his immediate task in the divine scheme expresses a firm conviction that there are facts of the matter and that speculation, when there is leisure for it, will take them as a touchstone. All religions have adherents whose primary convictions have this kind of directness. Indeed it may plausibly be argued that no religion could flourish unless some of its members found its basis self-evident. A church may be a broad-backed hippopotamus, in T. S. Eliot's arresting phrase, whose back sustains doubt, dissent and intricate theology and whose belly rests in the mud of matters temporal as well as spiritual. But it will sink unless some of its adherents find some of its doctrine simply and evidently true.

The current term for such pure conviction is usually faith. But the faithful, if philosophically *au fait*, might prefer "knowledge by acquaintance." Like Cartesians, they find some truths self-evident in the precise Cartesian sense of "known without proof or evidence." When Job exclaimed "I know that my redeemer liveth," despite having been smitten with enough plagues and boils to defy all reason, he was not merely affirming his faith but reporting what he now found clear and distinct. We need not share his belief to grant that he was not simply expressing his confidence.

To speak of self-evident facts of the matter and of knowledge by acquaintance, however, is to invite a straightforwardly relativistic retort: whatever the luminous confidence of the believer, there are many ideas of God, a great variety of believers, and no call for an interpreter to take sides. To understand the Book of Job or Sir Jacob Astley's prayer, we may need to identify the content of the beliefs expressed and to register their bedrock character but we need not consider their truth. If that involves mention of an unseen world and what it contains, then these are to be construed solely as internal objects of belief. It would of course be fascinating to know whether God did forget Sir Jacob and whether there is a god anyway, but, in the context of understanding, such curiosity is beside the point and talk of knowledge is gratuitous.

This relativist retort sounds neutral and preliminary, open to theist and atheist alike. Both might seem able to agree that truth is irrelevant to understanding, even if a vital topic for some other occasions. If then asked whether truth is also irrelevant to explanation, they might again agree that it is indeed irrelevant. Perhaps the atheist subscribes to a version of the hermeneutic tradition which holds that understanding a social world from within is both the alpha and the omega of explaining how it works, since referential beliefs are always to be construed internally whatever their content. Perhaps the theist espouses a strongly functionalist version of naturalism, which explains religion through the causal requirements of the social order but adds that it makes no difference to their social functions whether the beliefs are true or false. Such conflicting strategies make for fierce dispute about how to conceive of religion, for instance whether and how to contrast it with science or to relate it to a wider social world, but apparently without touching on the truth of primary claims to religious knowledge.

In that case it should be possible to divorce truth and method more generally. On the other hand there are many and conflicting claims to religious knowledge, starting with simple indicatives and ranging into the upper registers of refined theology. Questions of truth soon become nuanced, as one comes to wonder first whether "knowledge" has a logic relevant to all religious belief and practice, then whether "truth" is univocal between rationalists and mystics and then how exactly different religions are in competition, especially given ecumenical hopes that all are in search of the same god. But the day of judgment awaits and will settle these matters, unless, of course, atheists were right all along. On the other hand there are questions of method, chiefly to do with understanding and explanation, whether they complement one another and, if they conflict, which deserves to prevail.

To fence the divorce, a thesis about symmetry suggests itself. In so far as understanding turns on whether religious belief and practice are rational, *the rationality of beliefs is independent of their truth*. In so far as explanation turns on how belief and practice relate to features of a wider context, *it makes no difference whether the beliefs to be explained are true or false*.

I propose to argue that even this preliminary and neutral-sounding relativism will not do. It is plausible enough, owing to the murky state of play in philosophy of natural and social science, where naturalism has been trying to annex hermeneutics on favorable terms. But, when these alarums and excursions are surveyed coolly, we shall find that no part of the symmetry thesis holds. Consequently the stronger forms of relativism, which come closer to denying the existence of religious knowledge, have more to be said for them. But that is finally because questions of objective truth and falsity always matter – good news, I hope, for theists and atheists and a call for an apologia from agnostics.

NATURALISM AND HERMENEUTICS

Before starting in earnest at ground level, I should say an initial word about how I shall take "naturalism" and "hermeneutics." Naturalism cashes in as an ontological claim, memorably stated by La Mettrie: "Man is not fashioned out of a more precious clay. Nature has used only one and the same dough, in which she has merely varied the leaven." The dough need not be, as La Mettrie supposed, brutely physical. The crux is only that whatever the natural world is made of, the human world is made of too and hence that whatever method is suited to knowledge of nature is, with local variations no doubt, suited to the human and social parts of nature. In the Enlightenment mainline the method is one of causal explanation which proceeds by identifying laws of nature and applying them to the initial conditions of what is to be explained. But that leaves room for dispute about whether these laws involve necessity and of what sort. It also leaves room for a dissenting view that the moving force of the natural world is more particular – causal mechanisms, for instance. The unifying theme is that a single method of explanation, worked out for natural science, will serve across the board.

"Hermeneutics" will stand for an even looser set of prescriptions, premised on the thesis that the dough of the human world is action and that actions must be understood from within. Here too there is room for dispute between those who insist on the individual and subjective character of action, those who stress its intersubjective and contextual character and those who hold out for a dynamic or dialectic in the unfolding of history. Relatedly there is also dispute about the analysis of action and whether to treat it as the product of beliefs and desires or to regard it as the embodiment of rules and practices. Then again, although what counts is the *meaning* of action, in some sense of that nimble term, it may or may not be a shrewd move to gloss "meaning" as "rationality." In general, however, "meaning is the category which is peculiar to life and to the historical world" (Dilthey, 1926, vol. viii, p. 224), and I shall leave any questions about the exact peculiarities room to emerge.

Discussion of relativism is thus to be set against a background of argument about the relation of explanation (*Erklären*) to understanding (*Verstehen*). Roughly speaking, naturalists seek finally to explain, although they may allow understanding as a useful heuristic device; whereas hermeneuticists seek finally to understand, although they may regard the scientific practice of explanation as of special interest on the way. There are relativists on both sides of this argument and we should bear their differences in mind when considering the merits of compromises between naturalism and hermeneutics. The relativizing of truth is a different exercise depending on whether one tries finally to explain religion externally to religious belief and practice or to understand it internally to its own processes.

RELATIVIZING OBJECTS OF BELIEF

Meanwhile let us start at ground level with Astley's prayer from the front. The front line of religion does not consist only of warriors like Sir Jacob, ready to die by the sword in some crusade or *jihad*. Peaceful conviction is common, I am happy to say, and tolerance is often an option. But no one in the front line will grant that God is a purely internal object of belief. Astley's prayer is couched in a typically objective mode and has a firmly external address. So even a modest hermeneutic suggestion that we understand the prayer without worrying about truth threatens a tension between interpreter and subject. One asks whether a kind of understanding which is neutral about truth can reproduce a human world where claims to truth are primary.

To sharpen this question, consider a parallel one about perception. Can we understand what is in a perceiver's mind when he looks about him, without needing to check his claims about what he perceives against the independent and objective facts of the world? There has been a persistent tendency to say that understanding cannot be governed by knowledge of the facts, because we have no access to objects which bypass concepts and ways of thinking. Percepts without concepts are blind, and concepts belong to conceptual webs which are not neutral between individuals or, at any rate, between groups. Two influential reasons for treating objects of perception as a species of internal object are especially germane to the relativizing of religious "knowledge." One is the pragmatist contention that the mind is always active in constructing what passes for knowledge and hence that "facts" are always theory-dependent. To discover what someone perceives, one must penetrate a web of beliefs – a fabric of varying shades of gray, a body of beliefs which never face the tribunal of experience singly (e.g. Quine, 1961). To discover what someone perceives is to reconstruct what is itself an active construction, aimed at making overall sense of experience. There is no independent way the world is. The world is no particular way prior to all interpretation – an epistemological point interestingly reinforced by the findings of psychology, linguistics and anthropology.

The other reason for internalizing the objects of perception stems from one reading of Wittgenstein. Here objects in the external world are made subordinate to shared rules of judgment, and sensory objects in inner space drop out altogether. The argument from analogy is rejected as a solution to the problem of Other Minds. Inductive inferences from physical behavior to mental causes of behavior are replaced with interpretative accounts of what a person is (to be taken as) doing in a social context. To discover what someone perceives is first to understand the practices constituting and regulating the "game" of perceptual judgment. Thereafter behavior comes into particular identifications of belief, in that the practices connected with judgments of perception are functional in keeping us fed and in steering us round cats on mats. But the behavior is, by now, action and has a meaning which derives from a shared knowledge of "how to go on."

Pragmatist and Wittgensteinian lines are ambiguous about whether there are still raw cats on untheorized mats, independent of all concepts and "games." If so, however, they presumably matter no more than Kantian *Dinge an sich*, once the old dualisms of concept and object, meaning and experience, have been rejected. The physical objects which feature centrally in our stories and practices are by now, as Quine puts it, "irreducible posits, comparable epistemologically to the gods of Homer," and differing from those gods "only in degree and not in kind," since "both sorts of entities enter our conception only as cultural posits" (Quine, 1961, section 6, paragraph 4). In that case reconstructing a perceived world from within should not need an external test of truth for posits and practices.

Such anti-realist accounts of perception are relativist but, at first sight, only in the neutral-sounding sense that percepts without concepts are blind. To make them relativist in earnest it has to be added that concepts are always revisable and language-games radically variable because there are no unnegotiable external constraints. Yet even the neutral-sounding thesis conflicts with the realism embedded in everyday judgments of perception. That is very plain to Jack Sprat who eats no fat and his wife who eats no lean. They know a bit of bacon when they see one. Bacon is no more a "posit" for them than God was for Sir Jacob Astley. An interpretative line can try to accommodate these blunt realists by noting their fervent commitment to God and bacon and tracing its central role in their theory and practice. But there is still an incipient conflict: for Astley and the Sprats, God and bacon are prior to interpretation.

How far can we extend the parallel between perceptual and religious experience? Here the tension between naturalism and hermeneutics comes to the fore, with a resulting difference in what is involved in taking relativism seriously. Naturalists are likely to distinguish sharply between God and bacon. They need not be realists but, if they are, they will side with the Sprats in denying that bacon is theory-dependent and then offer a realist philosophy of science, where nature is an independent test of what it is rational to believe about nature. Equipped with an ontology which includes laws or mechanisms, they can proceed to a causal theory of perception, which explains belief that there is bacon on the plate as the effect of bacon on the plate. (Notice, however, that belief in unicorns cannot be explained as the effect of unicorns.) What, then, about God? Here realists divide, but one option which leads to a strong version of relativism is to explain religious belief with the aid of the same realist ontology. Since gods do not feature among the real furniture of nature, the result is to make religious belief relative to whatever does. It becomes, for instance, a function of psychological needs or of the requirements of a social structure. This seems to me to involve a clear denial of the symmetry thesis. A first asymmetry is that belief in bacon is explained by the presence of bacon whereas a belief in unicorns is not explained by the presence of unicorns. A deeper asymmetry is that temporal and spiritual beliefs are, in principle, explained in radically different ways.

To avoid confusion, I stress that I am contrasting naturalism with hermeneutics and realism with idealism. Not all naturalists are realists; not all hermeneuticists are idealists, at any rate about nature as opposed to culture. Moreover, even naturalists who are realists will often give religion more rope than they allow to scientific beliefs because they recognize the case for charting religious belief and practice from within in the first instance. That postpones the moment when relativism must show its hand, and so gives the symmetry thesis more of a run. Also, since it gives hermeneutics a substantial first turn, it becomes harder to identify the litmus test which will finally force a choice in priority between explanation and understanding. But, since I would rather let these matters take shape as we proceed, I shall next flesh out a notion of understanding to serve as common ground for all idealists, whether or not they accept a naturalist case for the final primacy of explanation.

RATIONALITY: THEORETICAL AND PRACTICAL REASON

Since our topic is religious knowledge, rather than religion at large, it will save space if I am allowed to connect understanding with rationality forthwith: to understand claims to religious knowledge one must apply criteria of rationality. The idea behind this proposal is that religious belief makes sense of the world, seen and unseen, for the believers and makes sense of their actions, interactions and practices. Any method of understanding must reproduce this sense, along with its scheme of reasons for belief and action. The scheme may include mysteries, where reason yields to faith, and the believers themselves may be inclined to protest that the imposition of rational order distorts the intimacy of their experience, faith and communion with the divine. But mysteries can be approached only by setting them amid what is not mysterious, and even the believers can understand their own beliefs only by interconnecting them rationally. Hence the most promising clue to the meaning of religious belief and practice is to presume that they are, for the most part, rational. The crucial question, then, is what criteria of rationality they satisfy.

That may seem a hopelessly open question, especially given its relativist flavor. But, broadly, accounts of rationality take as primary either theoretical or practical reason. Theoretical reason analyzes relations among beliefs, tracing the ways in which some beliefs give ground for others, on the presumption that reason aims at truth. Inductive and deductive reasoning are the standard models, even if there is dispute about how exactly to construe them and how exhaustive they are. The strongly relativist suggestion here is that even these models may not be universal and that other more local criteria can be found, especially when it comes to what passes locally for religious knowledge. Practical reason, on the other hand, fastens on the rule-governed character of assertions, which, like any other actions, are to be found sense and meaning by identifying the rules which govern them. The making of claims to religious knowledge is an institutional practice, to be understood, like any other practice, by discovering how to go on when it is one's turn to play. The criteria of rationality for the god-game, like all games, are internal to the game and players and investigators alike need to identify the reasons thus licensed. Interestingly the god-game played by believers contains a second-order game played by theologians. But then many institutional games, from science to bureaucracy, contain games for theorists, planners and policy-makers. Despite the relativistic sound of that remark, however, it is not simply the self-contained character of practices which implies a strong form of relativism but the further proposition that institutions are subject only to such criteria of rationality as they themselves authorize.

Theoretical Reason

Take theoretical reason first. A strongly relativist case is much helped if the grounds for a belief can only be another belief, as is suggested by the pragmatist metaphor of "the web of belief" and the post-modernist tendency to take "discourses" as ultimate. The enticing implication is that, since there are no extra-theoretical facts, reality is internal to these webs or discourses. It threatens to subvert modern philosophy at its starting point by confronting today's Descartes with a malignant demon whose technology can create a "virtual reality," complete with semantic rules for finding one's way about in it. But it does not impress Jack Sprat and Sir Jacob, whose reasons for belief are firmly cast in an objective mode, where extra-theoretical facts can be reasons. Fat tastes bad and God will excuse a Christian soldier on a busy day: reality is not the limiting case of virtual reality. Can a strong relativism deny it?

The strong relativist tackles Sir Jacob first. To understand Ancient Greek beliefs about the gods we need to trace the reasoning involved and recognize that much of it rests on "facts." But, since there was no pantheon ensconced on the top of Mount Olympus, any Greek who cited such a "fact" could only be relying on a further belief. Neither the meaning nor the rationality of ancient claims to knowledge depend on their truth. Hence generally, *pace* Jack Sprat too, what evidently holds for the meaning and rationality of a belief, when the truth is not as claimed or the believer does not know it, also holds for all beliefs. The method of *Verstehen* is holistic and internal: what a statement means depends solely on its relation to other statements; whether a belief is rationally held depends solely on its relation to other beliefs.

Furthermore, the strong relativist adds, the internal relations involved need not be those of deductive and inductive reasoning.

Take any text by a mystic, for example this stanza on the Trinity by St. John of the Cross:

> There is one love in all three Persons:
> One lover all the Three provides;
> And the beloved is the lover
> Which in each of them resides.

It belongs to a coherent vision and cannot be understood out of context without the rest of the vision and an appreciation of the wider Christian tradition, within which the vision is, none the less, St. John's own. But it can be understood. There is no reason to doubt the translation from the sixteenth-century Spanish (by the twentieth-century poet, Roy Campbell). To understand it, we need to identify the vision and trace connections among its elements which owe little to formal reasoning. But we need not subscribe to the vision nor ask ourselves whether St. John saw truly. Rationality can take many forms, each internal to local constructions or schemes of meaning and rational justification.

In the second-order game of theology too there is intelligible but local reasoning, where arguments are won or lost by criteria which are locally objective but without external standing. For example, consider the Pauline text central to the current storm over the ordination of women in the Church of England:

> Let a woman learn in silence with all submissiveness. I permit no woman to teach or have authority over man; She is to keep silent. For Adam was formed first, then Eve; and Adam was not deceived, but the woman was deceived and became a transgressor. Yet woman will be saved by bearing children, if she continues in faith and love and holiness, with modesty.   (I *Timothy* 2:1)

St. Paul uses a reason-giving, discursive mode of address readily intelligible whether or not one accepts the alleged facts about Adam and Eve and grants that they would, if so, warrant his conclusion. It is no less objectively open to opponents to argue that the text is no longer authoritative, if it ever was, for instance because the Christian tradition is not a rock but a river. In this dispute about whether women can be priests in the sight of God, there is an objective question of where the better reasons reside. But the objectivity involved in establishing the stronger case and the judgment of how women stand in the sight of God is a relative objectivity. By all means speak of "religious knowledge" but do not forget to add a strongly relativist rider.

I find this beguiling yet radical relativism deeply misconceived. It is beguiling in its respect for Other Minds and its recognition that, individually and collectively, they do not all work in the same way. But it is premised on a symmetry thesis which is, I contend, contradicted by any claim to be able to identify these differences. To establish a "bridgehead" in understanding other minds, languages and cultures, we need common knowledge and not merely shared (or identifiably different) belief.[1]

The basic objection to a strong relativism is that reality is not transmuted into an internal, virtual reality by granting that percepts without concepts are blind. Think how English-speakers come to know that *Einhorn* is the German for "unicorn." Since it cannot be done with the aid of unicorns, it cannot belong among the first knowledge, which can only depend on shared percepts. This has often been argued and often disputed. It was argued, for instance, by St. Augustine in the passage from his *Confessions* (I.8) which Wittgenstein quotes and then sets about undermining at the start of *Philosophical Investigations*. Augustine maintains that the fundamental linguistic activity is naming and that the basis of communication is mutual acquaintance with what is named. This connects with his contention that no one ever teaches anyone anything, since the learner can only be shown the way to recognize what is already within him. However odd as a general thesis, it seems to me wholly persuasive for the first knowledge – a phrase which I use in echo of Descartes and the role played by *intuitus* in his First Philosophy. In this tradition the first knowledge is of things, but the mind is active in recognizing them. Concepts and percepts fuse without thereby cutting the mind adrift from reality. In this sort of account "God" functions squarely as a name.

Relativism is beguiling in its denial that we can have any such first knowledge. But can we do without it? That is not a question to be settled by empirical evidence. Consider Robin Horton's (1982) distinction between "primary theory" and "secondary theory" in the thought of all the cultures which he has studied. Primary theory "gives the world a foreground filled with middle-sized . . . enduring solid objects" and involves "two major distinctions among its objects: first that between human beings and other objects; and second, among human beings, that between self and others." It "really does not differ very much from community to community or culture to culture" and "it provides the cross-cultural voyager with his intellectual bridgehead." Secondary theory, by contrast, "admits startling differences in kind as between community and community, culture and culture," for example between Western mechanistic views of the world and the spiritualist world-view of an African community. The objects of secondary theory are typically "hidden," like spirits or particles, and the theory typically transcends the given primary world in order to make intelligible "disturbing" primary events "previously inexplicable, unpredictable and uncontrollable." "Once the causal regularities governing this hidden world have been stated, their implications for the world as described in primary-theoretical terms are spelled out by a process akin to translation" (Horton, 1982, pp. 228–30).

As empirical evidence, these observations are plainly open to reinterpretation. Horton autocratically furnishes the primary foreground with middle-sized objects for relativists to bump into, and I doubt if that will worry them. A transcendental argument is needed, to the effect that translation has to presuppose a common stock of primary furniture as cataloged in a universal primary theory. The intellectual bridgehead is not a contingent feature of the world but a precondition *a priori* of the possibility of cross-cultural voyages. I cite Horton, therefore, not as evidence that there are elephants in Africa (or in African cultures) but as an example of an anthropologist whose "primary theory" is theoretical without being relativistic. At the same time, however, his "secondary theory" accords the same status to particles as to spirits. Both are objects in the same sense of being referents within a scheme of explanation. Both are assigned to a "hidden" realm of reality, although, since secondary theories can vary between and within cultures, this assignment is presumably an internal matter of what a secondary theory is committed to. In upshot, if my Kantian gloss is accepted, theoretical reason can best resist relativism by advancing a transcendental argument for a primary, theory-laden knowledge that some perceptual judgments are true, while allowing variations in secondary theory which may or may not turn out to fuel a strong relativist case.

Practical Reason

Although secondary theory deals in "hidden" entities, like particles and spirits, whose virtue is that they make what is "disturbing" explicable, the relativist is quick to suspect them of being wholly, or holistically, internal objects. In that case what, if anything, anchors them? Here let us shift attention from theoretical to practical reason and the idea that secondary theories are anchored by communal rules which constitute the practices of a culture and so guide its actions, including assertions. This may seem a tendentious gloss on the standard notion of practical reason as, broadly, a set of propositions which imply that x is the right thing to do, but it would, I hope, be plausible if theoretical reason were made subordinate to practical. Judging and asserting then become rule-governed practices, to be understood by reference to a "form of life." On a strongly relativist view particles and spirits feature in different "games" but both sorts of game have a similar structure of constitutive and regulative rules.

The attraction of the analogy with games is that science also needs to be seen in institutional as well as in cognitive terms, and that not even theology is wholly cerebral, since it has its own institutions and is deeply tied to first-order religions which emphatically have theirs. In both science and religion, stylites need pillars and the pillars belong to practices; cognitive activity is bound to or even grounded in practical activity. But, if that is all there is to be said, the same goes for many other games – witchcraft, martial arts, Japanese flower-arranging, American football, democratic politics, the "peculiar institution" of slavery and any other culturally specific practice with constitutive rules and internal virtues. As Mary Douglas has skillfully argued, every successful kind of institution includes "a formula that grounds its rightness in reason and nature," as part of a cognitive process which is "at the foundation of the social order" yet "depends on social institutions" (Douglas, 1987, p. 45). The measure of success is a continued legitimacy manifested in a successfully regulated conformity.

The strongly relativist contention on the hermeneutic side of the dispute with naturalism is that there is indeed nothing more to say. "Reason" and "nature" take varied forms, each finally internal to a contingent and historical amalgam of cognition and practice. If the case were well made, recent naturalists would have tried to annex the core of hermeneutics at their peril. In recognizing the theory-dependence of facts and the institutional character of cognition, they would have created a post-modern vacuum cleaner which sucks in reason, nature and, indeed, God with ease. The mighty Paradigm removes all dust by digesting the carpet. Nor does it stop there. As in a cartoonist's whimsy, I fancy, it gets attached to itself and implodes. If so, we need to stop the rot.

STOPPING THE ROT

The obvious stopper for naturalists to apply, despite having allowed understanding the first bite, is to deny that explanation is merely one practice among others. Scientific realists are willing to explore the cognitive and institutional aspects of science from the inside but refuse to be talked out of realism in the process (e.g. Bhaskar, 1978 and 1979). This refusal may sound dogmatic in its insistence that realism wields ontological trumps in any discussion of epistemology, but now is not the moment to pursue it. Naturalists who are anti-realists seem to me to be in greater trouble, if they want a stopper too, once they have granted the theory-dependence of facts. They must either try for a Kantian thesis about the universal and unique character of rational cognition, I think, or be reduced to whistling to keep their post-modern spirits up. Presumably both kinds of naturalist will be realists of some sort about social institutions if they propose to use institutional structures as the explanation of cognitive structures. That at least slows their hermeneutic opponents down, although it may not finally stop them, since institutions are too intersubjective to make it easy for naturalists to end their story there.

Meanwhile what of the unseen worlds that feature in claims to religious knowledge? The corresponding options are either to construe at least some of the claims in the realist manner by making them turn on the truth of the matter, thus presumably allowing religion a "primary theory," or to construe them as an interpretation of the natural and human worlds which does justice to their spiritual texture. This second option sounds relativistic but, I shall contend, need not be if we are careful about the role of truth in the god-game.

Consider the game readiest to hand, this conference itself.[2] To understand our proceedings an observer would, of course, need to grasp the rules and practices of academia, so as to follow the rituals of intellectual exchange across disciplinary boundaries. But, if the participants returning home can report *solely* that the rituals were duly kept, including the closing address with its benedictions about progress made, the conference will have been a sham. We come together not for a potlatch but to seek the truth about claims to reli-

gious knowledge. The truth may verily be that there is no such thing
as religious knowledge. The truth may verily be that there is no such
thing as religious knowledge. If so, however, that would be the truth
which we are seeking, even though it might be embarrassing to find
it. No doubt the final communiqué will say little about findings. But
it cannot be silent about the seeking. All who participate in good faith
must care for knowledge about religious knowledge. Those who
depart no wiser because they sought no wisdom may have enjoyed a
potlatch generously provided by our hosts but will have been
playing a different game, that of taking a holiday on expenses.

I stress that the conference is a truth-seeking game in an open-
minded sense which lets atheists or agnostics hold out for the falsity
or undecidability of claims to religious knowledge. So, too, skeptics
can attend meetings of the Sherlock Holmes Society. But they need to
care. In that example what they need to care about is a fictional world
and anyone who sincerely believes in Sherlock Holmes is no doubt
expelled. (The poor fellow would be like the houseparty guest
described by Saki, who fails to realize that dirty jokes must be told to
all the other guests privately one at a time so as to avoid shocking
public opinion.) This conference, however, is not at or about 221B
Baker Street. Its question is, in effect, whether everything worth
saying about "religious knowledge" can be said without inquiry into
the implications of removing the quotation marks. If it can, I submit,
the conference will have been a sham.

The symmetry thesis was that the truth or falsity of religious
beliefs is irrelevant both to assessing their rationality (*Verstehen*)
and to tracing their causal origin (*Erklären*). My closing comment
is entirely general. The irreducibly theoretical character of
primary theory implies neither symmetry. It has no such implication for perceptual judgments, as noted earlier. When a man
claims to have seen a unicorn in the garden, there is an unavoid-
able question of whether to summon a psychiatrist for the man or
a zookeeper for the unicorn. This can sometimes be delayed, since
he might have good reasons on a particular occasion, even
though there are no unicorns. But simple perceptual judgments in
general have mostly to be true if we are to establish what can
count as a good reason for them when they are false and thus
strike a balance of probabilities when we do not know whether
they are true or false. This is the nub of the "bridgehead" argument, which also implies that there is no symmetry in the kind of
causal connection involved in sending for a psychiatrist to treat a

disorder and sending for a zookeeper because the belief was caused by a unicorn.

The symmetry thesis remains very plausible, however, where uncertainty is endemic. Not only for advanced science but also for social theory, ethics, aesthetics and political philosophy, a deep agnosticism seems only prudent, at least for purposes of understanding and explaining beliefs. Religion is a splendidly symptomatic case because it makes no sense without its ontologies and its ontologies seem so definitely internal to its cognitive schemes. But here, as in the other realms, one must lay one's bets. If Sir Jacob Astley has no good reason to believe in God, then he needs a psychiatrist or his group of believers needs a structural explanation. If he has good reasons, then he needs, at worst, a theologian and the group can enjoy their elementary form of the religious life in peace. If we cannot decide whether he has good reason or not, we shall not know which route to take. But we are then also in doubt about how to understand the belief and in doubt whether it needs explaining. There is no implication that doubt warrants a symmetrical approach. We are merely hesitating which side of the asymmetry to come down on. To come down is to bet where the truth lies.

CONCLUSION

To arrive at reasoned conclusions about relativism and religious knowledge, we must proceed in two steps. The first is to identify some claims to religious knowledge. Whatever one says finally about the relation of understanding to explaining, this is a task for understanding. The claims have to be identified from within and this involves locating their supporting reasons so as to discriminate between competing interpretations. Hermeneutic circles lie in wait: to identify what Other Minds think real, one must know what they think rational and *vice versa*. To break in, we need to presuppose a universal primary theory and universal criteria of theoretical reason – a set of common beliefs which make common sense of a common world. There has to be at least one metanarrative. But, since the set need not include shared religious beliefs, the location of supporting religious reasons threatens a further circle. Here the entry is a universal notion of the search after truth: believers must be found reasons which, if true, are good reasons for beliefs about the facts of the unseen world. The first step takes us as far as we find good reasons for going, with scope for dispute among the voyagers about how far that is.

Thus far strong relativism has no purchase. The first step starts with universal criteria. Even if it extends into areas where local reasoning is at work, it still allows nothing stronger than a weak relativism. For example it may be that much of Islamic fundamentalism is held in place by appeal to the authority of a particular reading of the Koran. Without accepting that reading, one can still recognize that, were it authoritative, it would justify what depends on it. Strong relativism does not get its chance until the second step.

At the second step the path divides. Naturalists want causal explanations for the beliefs and practices, so far identified by finding their internal sense. Strong relativists among them will locate the causes in external structures, usually those of the surrounding social system or of the unconscious. Although I would be happy to dispute the merits of naturalism on another occasion, here I point out only that this strong form of relativism is squarely at odds with the symmetry thesis. It involves rejecting the believers' own explanation of their beliefs, since to hold reasoned beliefs about the unseen world is to deny that they are effects of structures, social or unconscious. Conversely, no one who shares such beliefs can consistently be a strong relativist. A strong relativist program must reject the symmetry thesis.

Hermeneuticists, who give understanding the omega as well as the alpha of the task, are content to make sense of religious beliefs and practices from the inside. Strong relativists among them will stress the relativity of the local criteria of sense and refer them to wider beliefs and practices of, no doubt, ultimately merely local authority too. Again this is squarely at odds with the symmetry thesis, since it involves rejecting the believers' understanding, which relates firmly to an unseen world. Conversely no convinced believer can espouse a version of hermeneutics which either leaves belief and practice up in the air or ties them solely to further beliefs and practices.

Whether strong relativism is nevertheless true in one or other version is a further question. It turns on whether any claims to religious knowledge are true. This is a question of substance, not of method, even if reflections on method and epistemology can help us lay our bets. Such reflections may assist in deciding, for instance, whether to construe the unseen world as a second world or as a revelation of aspects of this world. Comparison with questions about particles can even bear on how to regard spirits and *vice versa*. But, in the end, bets must be laid because what one says finally about the omega of explanation or understanding depends on them. My own bet, lest I seem furtive, is that the truth lies in a rapprochement between humanism and the sort of theology which takes the unseen world as a reading of spiritual truths about this world. In that case there is religious knowledge and, even if I am agnostic in most religious company, I hold no brief for any serious relativism.

That would not satisfy Sir Jacob Astley, I fear. He fought the good fight until clubbed to death with his wooden leg in the Drogheda massacre ten years later. I hope that God did not forget him. Meanwhile, laying my agnostic bets with half an eye to Pascal's wager, I commend the more nervous prayer which can be found on the tombstone of Martin Elginprod in an English church-yard. It strikes a properly anxious note for a discussion of religious knowledge.

> Here lie I beneath this sod.
> Have mercy on my soul, Lord God,
> As I would do were I Lord God
> and Thou poor Martin Elginprod.

Notes

1. In what follows I am relying on the line deployed in "Reason and Ritual" (Hollis, 1969) and "The Limits of Irrationality" (1970) (both in Wilson, 1970), "The Social Destruction of Reality" (in Hollis and Lukes, 1982), "Reasons of Honour" (1986) and chapter 11 of *The Cunning of Reason* (Hollis, 1988).
2. The James Montgomery Hester Seminar, 1992. See p. xiv.

References

Bhaskar, R. (1978) *A Realist Theory of Science* (Brighton: Harvester).
—— (1979) *The Possibility of Naturalism* (Brighton: Harvester).
Dilthey, W. (1926) *Gesammelte Werke*, edited by B. Groethuysen (Stuttgart: Teubner Verlag).
Douglas, M. (1987) *How Institutions Think* (London: Routledge & Kegan Paul).

Hollis, M. (1969) "Reason and Ritual," in Wilson (1970).
—— (1970) "The Limits of Irrationality," in Wilson (1970).
—— (1986) "Reasons of Honour," Presidential Address, *Proceedings of the Aristotelian Society*, LXXXVII, pp. 1–19.
—— (1988) *The Cunning of Reason* (Cambridge, Cambridge University Press).
Hollis, M. and Lukes, S., eds (1982) *Rationality and Relativism* (Oxford: Blackwell).
Horton, R. (1982) "Tradition and Modernity Revisited," in Hollis and Lukes, eds, pp. 201– 60.
Quine, W.V.O. (1961) "Two Dogmas of Empiricism," in *From a Logical Point of View* (New York: Harper & Row).
Wilson, B. R. (1970) *Rationality*, Oxford: Blackwell.
Wittgenstein, L. (1953) *Philosophical Investigations* (Oxford: Blackwell).

3

Religious Pluralism and Religious Relativism

Philip L. Quinn

The world presents us with a rich diversity of systems of religious belief. These systems make what seem to be competing and incompatible claims to truth. At least some of the adherents of each system appear to be perfectly rational in having the religious beliefs they do. What are we to make of this situation? In a recent discussion Joseph Runzo outlines six possible responses to the conflicting truth-claims of the world's religions.[1] Naturalism holds that all religions are mistaken. Religious Exclusivism maintains that only one world religion is correct and all the others are mistaken. Religious Inclusivism contends that only one world religion is fully correct but others contain some of the truth of the one correct religion. Religious Subjectivism claims that each world religion is correct in the sense that it is good for those who adhere to it. Religious Pluralism asserts that ultimately all world religions are correct, each offering a different salvific path and partial perspective on a single transcendent reality. And Religious Relativism argues that at least one, and probably more than one, world religion is correct and that the correctness of a religion is relative to the world-view of its community of adherents. Is there a good reason to prefer one of these responses to all its rivals?

Runzo argues against Naturalism, Exclusivism, Inclusivism and Subjectivism. I would like to defend Inclusivism against his criticism on some future occasion. On the present occasion my only concern is with his treatment of Pluralism and Relativism. Though he finds genuine merit in Pluralism, Runzo argues for the superiority of Relativism. Drawing on an account of truth relative to a conceptual schema he had set forth in earlier work, he proposes a version of Religious Relativism that does not, as he sees it, have the defects of Religious Pluralism.[2] My aim in this paper is to contest that conclusion. More precisely, I shall argue that Runzo's brand of Religious Relativism is inferior to John Hick's brand of Religious Pluralism. To my mind, a comparison of these two philosophers is apt to be illuminating because their views have a lot in common. But I shall try to show that, to the extent that they differ, Runzo's views are apt to be misleading.

The essay is divided into three parts. In the first section I give a brief sketch of relevant aspects of Hick's Religious Pluralism. This is a complex religious interpretation of religions that he has been working out over a number of years in a variety of publications. In my opinion, the best formulation of the position to have appeared in print so far occurs in the published version of his Gifford Lectures, *An Interpretation of Religion*, and in two papers published in the previous year.[3] So it is this mature version of Hick's position that is the object of my sketch. Next, in the second section of the essay, I give a somewhat more detailed exposition of Runzo's Religious Relativism, making use of both his book, *Reasons, Relativism and God*, and a more recently published paper. Finally, in the third section, I turn to the task of critically evaluating Runzo's Relativism and comparing it to Hick's Pluralism.

HICK'S PLURALISM

According to Hick, what the great religious traditions have in common is that each offers a path to salvation, which involves a transformation of human existence from self-centeredness to reality-centeredness. As far as we can tell, all of these traditions are of roughly equal effectiveness in producing this transformation. This suggests the hypothesis that a single ultimate reality "is being differently conceived, and therefore differently experienced, and therefore differently responded to from within our different religio-cultural ways of being human" (PS, p. 370). Speaking in Kantian terms, we may describe this ultimate reality as the Real *an sich* or the noumenal Real. It does not possess the features typically attributed to ultimate reality by the great religious traditions. Thus, for example, "it cannot be said to be one or many, person or thing, conscious or unconscious, purposive or nonpurposive, substance or process, good or evil, loving or hating" (*IR*, p. 350). This does not mean that there is nothing we can say about the Real *an sich*; it falls under certain purely formal concepts such as the concept of being beyond the scope of other than purely formal concepts. But, Hick insists, "the other than purely formal concepts by which our experience is structured must be presumed not to apply to its noumenal ground" (PS, p. 371). Hence the noumenal Real must be presumed not to fall under the other than purely formal concepts that shape the thought and experience of the great religious traditions.

There are in Hick's ontology, in addition to the noumenal Real, various tradition-specific phenomenal manifestations of it. Thus, "when we speak of a personal God, with moral attributes and purposes, or when we speak of the non-personal Absolute, Brahman, or of the Dharmakaya, we are speaking of the Real as humanly experienced: that is, as phenomenon" (*IR*, p. 246). There are therefore several phenomenal Reals, all of which are appearances or manifestations of the same noumenal Real. Allah is the phenomenal Real of Islam; Brahman is the phenomenal Real of advaitic Hinduism. And because both of them are manifestations of the Real *an sich*, neither is an illusion. On a naturalistic interpretation of religion, according to which there is no noumenal Real, the various phenomenal Reals of the religious traditions would be illusory because they would reduce to purely human projections. But on Hick's hypothesis, which postulates the existence of the noumenal Real in order to provide a religious interpretation of religion, the phenomenal Reals of the religious traditions will be "joint products of the universal presence of the Real and of the varying sets of concepts and images that have crystallized within the religious traditions of the earth" (PS, p. 372). So Hick's Religious Pluralism is pluralistic because it postulates a plurality of phenomenal Reals, all of which are partly human constructions. And it is religious because it also postulates a single noumenal Real, the Real *an sich*, which is the transcendent ground of the phenomenal Reals of the great religious traditions and insures that they are not mere human fabrications.

This view is, of course, an alternative and rival to the main lines of self-understanding within the great religious traditions. As one of its perceptive defenders acknowledges, it proposes "a revisionist conception of religions and religious diversity."[4] Many if not most members of the great religious traditions would object to the claim that what they take to be the ultimate religious reality is no more than one phenomenal Real among many. For example, an ordinary Christian theist who grasped the distinction between phenomena and noumena would be likely to insist that the noumenal Real, and not just its manifestations in Christian experience, is a personal God or, at least, that the noumenal Real is closely analogous to one or more human persons. Hick does what he can to accommodate such views, but the logic of his position does not allow him to do much. He recognizes that literal and analogical language about objects of religious worship or meditation always intends to be about the noumenal Real itself, but he holds that such language actually functions mythologically with respect to the noumenal Real. As he sees it, "we speak mythologically about the noumenal Real by speaking literally or analogously about its phenomenal manifestations" (*IR*, p. 351). And, according to the definition he proposes, "a statement or set of statements about *X* is mythologically true if it is not literally true but nevertheless tends to evoke an appropriate dispositional attitude to *X*" (*IR*, p. 348). All Hick can concede to the ordinary Christian theist is that it is mythologically but not literally true that the noumenal Real is personal. Similarly, all he can concede to advaitic Hindus is that it is mythologically but not literally true that the noumenal Real is non-personal.

Hick's Religious Pluralism, as I understand it, is thus committed to a number of truth-claims about whether various objects of religious concern are personal or impersonal. All of them are claims to literal and non-relative truth. It is not true that the noumenal Real is personal, and it is not true that the noumenal Real is impersonal. Of course both these statements are mythologically "true," but that only means that, in the right contexts, they tend to evoke appropriate attitudes toward the noumenal Real. However, it is literally true that the noumenal Real appears or manifests itself to some people, for example, Christian theists, as personal, and it is also literally true that the noumenal Real appears or manifests itself to other people, for instance, advaitic Hindus, as impersonal. These diverse appearances or manifestations are the diverse phenomenal Reals of those two traditions, partly products of their conceptual schemas. Hence it is true that the phenomenal Real of Christianity is personal and that the phenomenal Real of advaitic Hinduism is impersonal. It is important to be clearly aware that these last two claims could both be true because they do not attribute incompatible properties to a single entity but instead refer to two distinct phenomenal entities.

Needless to say, Hick's position has generated considerable controversy and will no doubt continue to do so for quite a while.[5] I do not propose to give it a thorough critical appraisal in this paper. I want instead to address the question of whether it has defects that could be remedied by moving to some form of religious relativism. So I next turn my attention to the version of that doctrine I consider the most sophisticated currently available.

RUNZO'S RELATIVISM

According to Runzo, both truth and phenomenal reality are relative to socially entrenched conceptual schemas that mark out different world-views. He spells out the details of this conceptual relativism in terms of three general principles. Let us think of a possible world order as a possible totality of perceived reality for perceivers who possess the same conceptual schema. In other words, a possible world order is a possible totality of phenomenal reality for perceivers who share a single schema. The Diversity Principle asserts that "there exist distinct and mutually incompatible world-view conceptual schemas, and each schema delimits a set of possible world orders which is incompatible with the set of possible world orders delimited by any other, mutually incompatible schema" (*RG*, p. 58). For Runzo, a conceptual schema determines a set of possible phenomenal realities. Which of these possibilities is actual for those who operate with a certain schema is then settled by the interaction of their schema with noumenal reality to produce their experiences of phenomenal reality.

The remaining two principles are meant to effect the double relativization of truth and phenomenal reality to conceptual schemas. The Dependency Principle, which does the job for truth, tells us that "the truth of any statement, P, depends, in part, on the conceptual schema from within which P is formulated and/or assessed" (*RG*, p. 59). In order to block the application of the Dependency Principle to itself that would render its relativization of truth self-stultifying, we must stipulate, as Runzo acknowledges earlier in his discussion (*RG*, p. 39) but seems to have forgotten when he formulated the principle, that the principle does not apply to all statements but only to the statements in a restricted class to which it itself does not belong.

To grasp the Pluralist Ontology Principle, which does the job of relativizing phenomenal reality to conceptual schemas, we need to understand two other ideas. Let us say that a world-view conceptual schema adequately delimits a set of possible world orders only if it offers those who operate with it the possibility of sufficient diversity and fineness of discrimination in their perceptual experience to enable them to survive and function successfully. And let us define an actual world as consisting of both an actual world order, which is a phenomenal reality, and the one noumenal reality, things in themselves, whatever they may be. The Pluralist Ontology Principle claims that "each, and only each, distinct world-view conceptual schema, which adequately delimits a set of possible world orders, delimits an actual world, and no two schemas delimit identical actual worlds" (*RG*, p. 60). Hence, according to Runzo's conceptual relativism, there is a plurality of actual worlds. But, as he insists, "since the one noumenal reality, by definition, is what it is apart from any mind-imposed perspective or construction, the difference between *actual* worlds just is the difference between the phenomenal realities of those worlds" (*RG*, p. 60). In other words, all actual worlds share the same noumenal reality and differ only in their phenomenal realities, and so differences in actual worlds reduce to differences in actual world orders.

Runzo claims that it follows from these principles "that, corresponding to this plurality of actual worlds, there is not just one set of truths, but a plurality of mutually incompatible sets of truths" (*RG*, p. 61). So he says that "a conceptual relativist *definitively* holds that truth is relative in the strong sense of there being mutually incompatible, yet individually adequate, sets of conceptual-schema-relative truths" (*RG*, p. 62). And he repeats this claim almost word for word in a later paper, asserting there that "a conceptual relativist definitively holds that, corresponding to differences of world-view, there are mutually incompatible, yet individually adequate, sets of conceptual-schema-relative truths" (GC, p. 351). Such sets, he explains, will be incompatible "because at least some truth-claims in each set will be false, or logically inconsistent, or simply of indeterminate truth value, in an opposing set" (*RG*, p. 62). In short, there are plural and incompatible schema-relative truths because true statements are about reality and there are, at the phenomenal level, plural and incompatible schema-relative realities.

The application of general conceptual relativism to the religious realm yields Runzo's Religious Relativism. Just as there is more than one phenomenal reality, more than one actual world, so also there is more than one phenomenal ultimate reality, more than one phenomenal divine reality. As Runzo sees it, "talk about 'The' God of history is talk about a phenomenal reality" (*RG*, p. 240). Thus

"The" God of history is not the noumenal Real but one of many phenomenal Reals. But it would be a mistake to think that "The" God of history is illusory. As Runzo observes, "just as there is nothing unreal about nuclear weapons or pains or piano concertos because they are part of phenomenal reality, 'The' God of history, 'The' God one confronts, is not less real, if He exists, just because He is not in the category of the noumenal" (GC, p. 356). Of course since "The" God of history is phenomenal, He is the joint product of the noumenal Real, whatever it may be, and some theistic world-view conceptual schema that delimits the actual world to whose phenomenal actual world order He belongs. His is, then, a schema-relative reality, and there will be schema-relative truths about Him. The same will be the case for other phenomenal Reals, including presumably both those that belong to the actual world orders of alternative theistic world-view conceptual schemas and those that belong to the actual world orders of non-theistic world-view conceptual schemas. They too will be schema-relative realities, not illusions, and there will also be schema-relative truths about them. Since it seems likely that world-view conceptual schemas that are embedded in the great religious traditions satisfy the pragmatic condition of adequately delimiting a set of possible world orders, precisely because those traditions have stood the test of time, Religious Relativism "allows for the likelihood that more than one of the conflicting sets of *specific* truth-claims, which adherents of the differing world religions themselves regard as vital to their faith, is correct" (GC, p. 357). But, it must be added, correctness here amounts to no more than schema-relative truth about schema-relative phenomenal realities.

It is, I think, of considerable interest to compare the kinds of things Hick and Runzo are prepared to relativize. For both of them, the noumenal Real is immune from relativization. Both recognize a plurality of phenomenal Reals. Hick relativizes them to religious traditions conceived of as streams of thought and experience, and Runzo does much the same by relativizing them to socially shared conceptual schemas and the experience of those who operate with them. But Runzo also relativizes truth, and Hick does not. For Runzo there are schema-relative truths about schema-relative phenomenal realities; Hick, as far as I can tell, is committed only to schema-independent literal truths about the plurality of phenomenal Reals. Is Runzo's second relativization a smart move? I shall next argue that its chief effect is to get him into philosophical trouble.

RELATIVISM VERSUS PLURALISM

By definition, it will be recalled, Runzo's conceptual relativist holds that there are mutually incompatible schema-relative truths. As one reviewer of Runzo's book has noted, it suffers from "an elusive abstractness endemic to talk about alternative conceptual schemas."[6] It does not do very much by way of providing concrete examples of pairs of propositions or sentences that are plausible candidates for the status of incompatible truths. Can we find any such examples? This is a question that deserves an extended discussion.

Suppose someone tells us this: it is true that Jean is a female, and it is true that Jean is a male. Having ruled out the possibility that Jean is a hermaphrodite, we think we see that these are indeed incompatible truth-claims, and this leads us to think that one of them must be mistaken. Not so, we are told, because "Jean" in the first of them refers to Jean Simmons, the film actress, and "Jean" in the second refers to Jean Renoir, the film director. Now we see that both claims are true, but the illusion that they are incompatible has been dispelled. If the phenomenal Reals of different world-view conceptual schemas are diverse, there will be a similar illusion to dispel when we consider what purport to be incompatible truths about the phenomenal Real.

A Religious Relativist might say that it is true, relative to the Christian theist's conceptual schema, that the phenomenal Real is personal and that it is true, relative to the advaitic Hindu's conceptual schema, that the phenomenal Real is impersonal. So we have the following example of incompatible truths: the phenomenal Real is personal, and the phenomenal Real is impersonal. The former is true relative to the conceptual schema of Christian theism, and the latter is true relative to the conceptual schema of advaitic Hinduism. If all this is treated as a mere *façon de parler*, I have no objection to it. But there are better ways to describe the situation under consideration. Because the Religious Relativist has relativized phenomenal reality to conceptual schemas, there are two phenomenal Reals, not just one, for us to keep track of in our discussion. One is the phenomenal Real of Christianity, and the other is the phenomenal Real of advaitic Hinduism. The former is personal; the latter is impersonal. We can therefore accurately describe the situation by saying, as the Religious Pluralist does, that it is true that the phenomenal Real of Christianity is personal and that the phenomenal Real of advaitic Hinduism is impersonal. Since they are distinct phenomenal realities, there is no incompatibility in claiming that one of them is personal and the other impersonal. The truth of such claims is literal and non-relative truth. Once phenomenal reality has been relativized to conceptual schemas, a second relativization of truth about phenomenal reality is otiose.

Perhaps I can make this point clearer by constructing a parody of the Religious Relativist's argument. Suppose you and I are both staring at a large white wall. You are looking at it through red-tinted glasses, and I am looking at it through green-tinted glasses. Imagine an extreme relativist telling us that it is true, relative to you, that the visual field is red all over and it is true, relative to me, that the visual field is green all over. So here we have another example of incompatible truths: the visual field is red all over, and the visual field is green all over. The former is true relative to you; the latter is true relative to me. It is, I hope, obvious that this way of describing our situation is perverse. There are two visual fields under consideration, yours and mine. Your visual field is red all over, and my visual field is green all over. Being about distinct things, these claims are compatible. We can accurately describe the imagined situation by saying that it is true, literally and non-relatively, that your visual field is red all over and that my visual field is green all over. The appeal to person-relative truth is completely superfluous. Such talk is, at best, quite misleading.

So sentences or propositions about the diverse phenomenal Reals of different conceptual schemas will not yield examples in which it is useful to talk about mutually incompatible schema-relative truths. The alternative, of course, is to look for examples among the sentences or propositions that are about something that remains identical across world-view conceptual schemas. According to Religious Relativism, such a thing would be a noumenon, and the noumenon of religious interest is the noumenal Real. Are there mutually incompatible schema-relative truths about the noumenal Real?

Well, suppose a Religious Relativist says that it is true, relative to the Christian theist's conceptual schema, that the noumenal Real manifests itself as personal and that it is true, relative to the advaitic Hindu's conceptual schema, that the noumenal Real manifests itself as impersonal. The proposed example of incompatible truths will then be this pair: the noumenal Real manifests itself as personal, and the noumenal Real manifests itself as impersonal.

The former is true relative to the conceptual schema of Christian theism, and the latter is true relative to the conceptual schema of advaitic Hinduism. In both members of the pair "the noumenal Real" refers to the same thing, and so it cannot be said that the two claims are about different things. If there is only an illusion of incompatibility in this case, it will have to be dispelled in some other way.

Consider, by way of an analogy, an argument meant to show that there are incompatible place-relative truths. It begins with the claim that it is true, relative to Miami, that Wake Forest is to the north and that it is true, relative to Philadelphia, that Wake Forest is to the south. From this it is concluded that the following truths are incompatible: Wake Forest is to the north, and Wake Forest is to the south. The former is true relative to Miami but false relative to Philadelphia, and the latter is true relative to Philadelphia but false relative to Miami. Moreover, the referent of "Wake Forest" is the same in both claims, and so it cannot be said that the two claims are about different things. I consider this a contrived but acceptable way of talking about geographical relations in the eastern United States. If you and I met in the Miami airport and you remarked that Wake Forest is to the north, I would take you to speak truly because I would interpret you to mean that Wake Forest is to the north of here. If you and I met in the Philadelphia airport and you observed that Wake Forest is to the south, I would again take you to speak truly because I would interpret you to mean that Wake Forest is to the south of here. In both cases I would understand you to be committed to a proposition asserting that a spatial relation holds between Wake Forest and some other place. I would certainly not take you to be committed to the existence of two non-relational properties, being to the north and being to the south, such that Wake Forest possesses the former and not the latter relative to Miami and possesses the latter and not the former relative to Philadelphia. It seems to me that the whole story about the geographical relations in question can be told in terms of four non-relative truths about relations. It is true that Wake Forest is to the north of Miami and that Wake Forest is not to the south of Miami. And it is also true that Wake Forest is to the south of Philadelphia and that Wake Forest is not to the north of Philadelphia. Of course one thing cannot, leaving aside circumnavigation of the globe, be both to the north of and to the south of another. But one thing can be both to the north of a second and to the south of a third. Hence I think it promotes understanding to regard sentences that are alleged to express place-relative truths as abbreviations for sentences that express non-relative truths about spatial relations. In short, talk about place-relative truth is acceptable only because it can be analyzed away in terms of talk about non-relative truths about relations of geography.

The same thing is the case for schema-relative truths about manifestations of the noumenal Real. It is true that the noumenal Real manifests itself as personal in the Christian theist's conceptual schema, and it is true that the noumenal Real manifests itself as impersonal in the advaitic Hindu's conceptual schema. As I have indicated, Religious Pluralism is committed to both these claims or to very similar claims, and both are claims to non-relative truth. To say that it is true, relative to the Christian theist's conceptual schema, that the noumenal Real manifests itself as personal is to say nothing more than that it is true that the noumenal Real manifests itself as personal in the Christian theist's conceptual schema. And to say that it is true, relative to the advaitic Hindu's conceptual schema, that the noumenal Real manifests itself as impersonal is to say nothing more than that it is true that the noumenal Real manifests itself as impersonal in the advaitic Hindu's conceptual schema. Sentences that are alleged to express schema-relative truths about the noumenal Real are best seen as abbreviations for sentences that express non-relative truths about relations between the noumenal Real and various conceptual schemas. In other words, talk about schema-relative truths about the noumenal Real is acceptable only because it can be analyzed away in terms of talk about non-relative truths about relations between the noumenal Real and the schemas in which it manifests itself.

It may be granted, if only as an idealization, that the noumenal Real cannot both manifest itself as personal and manifest itself as impersonal in a single conceptual schema. But since it is committed to relativizing phenomenal reality to conceptual schemas, Religious Relativism must hold that the noumenal Real can manifest itself as personal in one conceptual schema and manifest itself as impersonal in another. It may at first glance seem that talk of the diverse manifestations of the noumenal Real involves attributing contrary properties to it. Upon analysis, however, it becomes clear that what this kind of talk really comes to is claiming that the noumenal Real stands in one relation to one conceptual schema and in another relation to another schema. There is no trace of incompatibility in this, and so once again the illusion is dispelled. If properly understood, talk of schema-relative truth is a harmless *façon de parler* because it is eliminable in favor of talk of non-relative truth about relations.

Up to this point in the argument, we have found no reason for having recourse to schema-relative truth. Runzo's second relativization therefore appears to be wholly superfluous. Let me conclude this part of the argument by attempting to give a general explanation of why this is not a deceptive appearance.

Suppose we start with two contrary properties, P and Q. It cannot be a non-relative truth, nor can it be true relative to a single schema, that one individual, a, has both P and Q. So if we wish to say both that a has P and that a has Q, we will be forced to say that it is true relative to one schema that a has P and lacks Q and true relative to another that a has Q and lacks P. But it can be a non-relative truth that one individual, a, has P and another individual, b, has Q. Hence if all we wish to say is that a has P and b has Q, we are not forced to appeal to schema-relative truth. Now, according to Religious Relativism, different schemas have different phenomenal Reals. All we wish to say is that a, the phenomenal Real of Christian theism, has P, the property of being personal and b, the phenomenal real of advaitic Hinduism, has Q, the property of being impersonal. Therefore the appeal to schema-relative truth is unnecessary.

Suppose we start with two relations, R and S, such that a single individual, a, cannot bear both R and S to a second individual, b, but can bear R to b and bear S to a third individual, c. It cannot be a non-relative truth, nor can it be true relative to a single schema, that a bears both R and S to b. So if we wish to say both that a bears R to b and that a bears S to b, we will be forced to say that it is true relative to one schema that a bears R but not S to b and true relative to another that a bears S but not R to b. But it can be a non-relative truth that a bears R to one individual, b, and also bears S to another individual, c. Hence if all we wish to say is that a bears R to b and a bears S to c, we are not forced to appeal to schema-relative truth. According to Religious Relativism, the noumenal Real bears diverse relations of manifestation to different conceptual schemas. All we wish to say is that a, the noumenal Real, bears R, the relation of manifesting itself as personal, to b, the Christian theist's conceptual schema, and bears S, the relation of manifesting itself as impersonal, to c, the advaitic Hindu's conceptual schema. Thus, once again, the appeal to schema-relative truth is unnecessary.

If properly understood as nothing more than a manner of speaking, talk about schema-relative truth can be harmless enough. However, it is not needed to tell the sober metaphysical truth about either the diverse ways in which the one noumenal Real manifests itself in different conceptual schemas or the diverse attributes of the several phenomenal Reals. For this purpose literal and non-relative truth suffices. Thus it is hard to see how Religious Relativism could have a competitive edge over Religious Pluralism. We must, therefore, scrutinize with care Runzo's reasons for thinking his Religious Relativism has merits that Hick's Religious Pluralism lacks. Runzo offers three such reasons.

The first is that "Religious Pluralism fails to adequately account for the necessary, central role of cognition in religious faith" (GC, p. 353). As Runzo sees it, "the *specific* cognitive content of one's faith is of paramount importance since it is precisely what delimits one's *specific* path to salvation/liberation" (GC, p. 354). In a brief reply, Hick correctly points out that there is no reason why a Religious Pluralist should want to deny that the different paths to salvation proposed by the great religious traditions are defined by their respective systems of belief. According to Pluralism there are several such paths, and all of them are, as far as we can tell, roughly equal in effectiveness. All the Pluralist wants to insist on is "that no one of the doctrinal systems taught by the great traditions is such that it is essential for salvation that one believe that system" (CC, p. 454). In terms of the prospects they offer for religious cognition or knowledge, Pluralism and Relativism seem to be on a par. Since both operate with a Kantian distinction between phenomenal and noumenal realms, both make it possible for each of the great traditions to have extensive and growing knowledge of its own phenomenal Real. But neither offers the prospect of extensive knowledge of the one noumenal Real. For Hick such knowledge would have to be restricted to truths that can be expressed in terms of purely formal concepts. The question for Runzo's Relativism is whether it holds that any tradition has more extensive access to truths about the noumenal Real.

In the course of setting forth his second objection to Pluralism, Runzo suggests an answer to this question, but it is not the answer one would antecedently have expected. The objection is that Pluralism treats conceptual diversity among the world religions as inconsequential and thereby detracts from the dignity of each distinct community of faith. Applied to Christianity, the charge is that

Pluralism "obviates the significance of the Christian understanding of a personal God as *somehow* correctly revealing the nature of Ultimate Reality in itself" (GC, p. 355). Since something that is personal could not be identical to something that is impersonal, Runzo takes it that "this Pluralist account entails that the monotheist's experience of a *personal* divine reality *cannot*, to that extent, correctly represent the nature of the Real in itself" (GC, p. 355). As we have seen, Hick accepts the consequent of this entailment. On his view the noumenal Real is not personal. Runzo will have to pay a high price if he asserts that, on the contrary, the noumenal Real is personal. If he makes this claim, he is committed to holding that theistic conceptual schemas provide privileged access to the nature of the noumenal Real, and this commitment would make him a theistic Exclusivist about the nature of the noumenal Real. It is this important issue that Hick raises but does not try to settle when, in his reply, he asks whether the difference between his view and Runzo's is "that the full pluralistic hypothesis extends to the non-theistic forms of religious experience whilst Runzo's relativism only covers the monotheisms" (CC, p. 454). If this is the real difference, it is Runzo's Relativism that does not acknowledge the equal dignity of all the great religious traditions. It defends the significance of the Christian understanding of a personal God as correctly revealing the nature of Ultimate Reality in itself by flatly denying the significance of the advaitic Hindu understanding of an impersonal Absolute as correctly revealing the nature of Ultimate Reality in itself. And, at this point at least, it collapses the distinction between the noumenal and the phenomenal by claiming that both the noumenal Real and the phenomenal Reals of theistic traditions are personal.

There is some irony in this charge, since Runzo accuses Hick's view of threatening to collapse that distinction. According to Runzo, the threat comes from the fact that the Pluralist holds that "the divine phenomena just *are* the divine noumenon *as* experienced by humans via their particular religio-cultural perspectives" (GC, p. 358). There can be no doubt that Hick has made claims much like this one. Even in his reply to Runzo, he asserts that "according to the pluralistic hypothesis the phenomenal manifestations of the Real, the divine *personae* and *impersonae*, are the noumenal Real as humanly experienced in terms of the various conceptual schemas" (CC, p. 454). But I take the fault here to amount to nothing worse than loose and careless talk. It is, I think, a holdover from a time, earlier in Hick's career, when he was trying to articulate his position in terms of the concept of experiencing-as that plays an important role in the work of the later Wittgenstein. In explaining this concept, Wittgenstein appeals to such things as the *gestalt* figure of the duck-rabbit, which can be seen as a duck or seen as a rabbit. Either way, however, the duck-rabbit figure is experienced; it is a phenomenal object. Reasoning by analogy, one would seem to be entitled to conclude that, when the noumenal Real is experienced as personal or experienced as impersonal, the noumenal Real is itself humanly experienced. But the logic of Hick's present Kantian position dictates, as Runzo clearly sees, that the noumenal Real cannot be humanly experienced. Only phenomenal realities, such as the several phenomenal Reals of the great religious traditions, are possible objects of human experience. Once this is granted, however, Hick's Pluralism can acknowledge the equal dignity of all the great traditions. The significance of the Christian understanding of a personal God and of the advaitic Hindu understanding of an impersonal Absolute is not that either understanding correctly reveals the nature of Ultimate Reality in itself. Neither of them does that because the noumenal Real is neither personal nor impersonal. But both of them are understandings of manifestations of the noumenal Real, and so the phenomenal Reals thus understood are both grounded in the one noumenal Real. Hence their significance derives from being so grounded, from making contact with the noumenal Real in a way that is salvific. And since Runzo's position is also Kantian in this respect, he cannot claim that the significance of either understanding is that it correctly reveals the nature of Ultimate Reality in itself unless he is prepared to say that some but not all of the conceptual schemas of the great traditions provide privileged access to the nature of the noumenal Real and thereby adopt an Exclusivist view of the nature of the noumenal Real. So Runzo's Relativism turns out to be no better than Hick's Pluralism at safeguarding the equal dignity of all the great religious traditions.

Runzo's third reason for preferring his Religious Relativism to Religious Pluralism is that the latter "is deficient insofar as it unintentionally undermines the sense of the reality of God" (GC, p. 355). This is an odd complaint for Runzo to lodge against Hick's brand of Pluralism, since it seems clear that they agree in thinking that the personal God of history is a phenomenal reality but not an illusion. In other words, this God is a phenomenal Real for one or more theistic traditions but is not the noumenal Real, the Real *an sich*. If this is not enough to support a robust sense of the reality of God, then Religious Relativism shares with Religious Pluralism the defect of undermining that sense unless Relativism is prepared to bolster the sense of the reality of God by claiming that the noumenal Real is personal. But, as we have just seen, such a turn to Exclusivism about the nature of the noumenal Real would bring with it other disadvantages. On this score, too, Runzo's Relativism turns out to be no better than Hick's Pluralism.

In the last paragraph of his reply to Runzo, Hick confesses he finds it "difficult to distinguish Runzo's Relativism from the Pluralism from which he wants to separate it" (CC, p. 454). If my analysis of the situation is correct, this is because the two views do not differ in substance but differ only in a manner of speaking. In addition, Runzo has so far offered no reason for preferring his Relativism to Hick's Pluralism that turns out, upon examination, to be a good reason for such a preference. In the light of these considerations, I think we are entitled to conclude that Runzo and Hick are not offering distinct religious interpretations of religion; what they have to offer is, as I see it, alternative formulations of a single interpretation. Of the two formulations, Runzo's is the more complicated on account of its appeal to schema-relative truth. Such talk of schema-relative truth is unnecessary because it is eliminable in favor of literal and non-relative truth. Therefore Hick's formulation is to be preferred on grounds of simplicity.

In concluding, let me return to Runzo's list of six possible responses to the conflicting truth-claims of the world's religions. Though I concede that it might ultimately turn out to be the correct response, I dismiss Naturalism from consideration because I share with Hick and Runzo the desire to work out a religious interpretation of religion. I also dismiss Subjectivism on account of its extreme individualistic bias. If the argument of this essay is on the mark, Pluralism and Relativism are not distinct views in the forms they assume in the work of Hick and Runzo. Hence the range of distinct options reduces to Exclusivism, Inclusivism and Pluralism. As I hinted in my introduction, I would like to be able in the long run to defend some version of Inclusivism. From this point of view, I see just one alternative on either side of my own position. On my right, I find the conservative and old-fashioned position, Religious Exclusivism; on my left, I find the radical and new-fangled position, Religious Pluralism. Being inclined by instinct toward the middle of the road, I invoke the principle of *virtus in medio*. Though I realize this is not much of an argument for the truth of Religious Inclusivism, it does, I think, speak volumes for its promise as a research program in comparative theology and philosophy of religion.[7]

Notes

1. Joseph Runzo, "God, Commitment, and Other Faiths: Pluralism vs. Relativism" (hereafter GC), *Faith and Philosophy* 5 (1988): 343–64. I shall make page references to GC parenthetically in the body of my text.
2. Joseph Runzo, *Reason, Relativism and God* (hereafter RG) (New York: St. Martin's Press, 1986). I shall make page references to RG parenthetically in the body of my text.
3. John Hick, *An Interpretation of Religion* (hereafter IR) (New Haven and London: Yale University Press, 1989); John Hick, "Religious Pluralism and Salvation" (hereafter PS), *Faith and Philosophy* 5 (1988): 365–77; and John Hick, "A Concluding Comment" (hereafter CC), *Faith and Philosophy* 5 (1988): 449–55. I shall make page references to IR, PS and CC parenthetically in the body of my text.
4. Sumner B. Twiss, "The Philosophy of Religious Pluralism: A Critical Appraisal of Hick and His Critics," *The Journal of Religion* 70 (1990): 543.
5. For recent criticism of Hick's Pluralism, see Paul J. Griffiths, "An Apology for Apologetics," *Faith and Philosophy* 5 (1988): 399–420, and Timothy R. Stinnett, "John Hick's Pluralistic Theory of Religion," *The Journal of Religion* 70 (1990): 569–88.
6. Thomas F. Tracy, "Review of *Reason, Relativism and God*," *Faith and Philosophy* 5 (1988): 462.
7. I am grateful to John Hick and Joseph Runzo for comments on a version of this essay that I read at the 1992 Pacific Regional Meeting of the Society of Christian Philosophers.

4

The Justificationist Roots of Relativism

I. C. Jarvie

Confronted with the diverse range of religious claims to truth one can affirm one of them, deny the rest, and thereby be a believer and a *non-relativist;* one can deny them all, and thereby be a non-believer and an *anti-relativist;* and one can affirm them all, each in its cultural place, without thereby being a believer: one is then a *relativist.* There are no other logical options. The two positions which interest me here are *relativism* and *anti-relativism.* At first glance they might seem symmetrical, or mirrors of one another: the relativist affirms what the anti-relativist denies. Yet beyond this simple relation of negation the two are as different as chalk and cheese. Relativism has a justificationist structure and an authoritarian epistemology to go with it. Anti-relativism, by contrast, can be formulated free from those deficiencies.

RELATIVISM AND JUSTIFICATION

Philosophers of religion (among others) fall into relativism during the search for foundations on which to rest the claims they make, a quest the late W. W. Bartley labelled "justificationism."[1] Consider the situation created by the existence of diverse and conflicting claims to knowledge and value. The conflicts appear to call for some adjudication. The adjudication device most commonly reached for in philosophy consists in comparing what were variously called the foundations, the bases, the grounds of the conflicting claims. Claims discovered to be resting on solid foundations were by that means justified. By their grounds shall ye justify them.

Many different justifying foundations for knowledge and value have been proposed in the past, among them Plato's Forms, the empiricist's impressions or sense-data, Descartes' clear and distinct ideas, Kant's *a priori* categories of the understanding, the principle of universalizability, utilitarianism – but these and others have been found wanting by contemporary philosophers, not to mention interested onlookers in anthropology, sociology, philosophy of science and elsewhere.[2] In the first third of this century the logical positivists hoped that empiricism plus the logical analysis of language would provide solid foundations from which to adjudicate on knowledge claims; they relegated value claims to unjustifiable matters of taste. Successor schools hoped that the analysis of the logical grammar of ordinary language would ground knowledge and value.

Ordinary or natural language was plainly a social institution, perhaps even the central and constitutive institution;[3] and, while clearly the result of human action, ordinary language was not the result of human design, so it was in some sense transcendent. The search for a justifying foundation for knowledge and value claims in the analysis of ordinary language could not then stop at the level of language as such but had to be pushed back to the society which used the language and which the language helped constitute. The foundation for a knowledge claim or a moral principle was to be sought in the *society* in which the claim or principle was uttered and endorsed.[4] Not ordinary language but the forms of life constituted around ordinary (or natural) languages were the site for the ultimate justification of claims.

But this way of adjudicating between competing knowledge and value claims fails. There are many societies or forms of life. If we locate the foundations for competing knowledge claims or value claims in society, we end up with at least as many foundations as societies. Thus the possibility of equally well-founded but conflicting claims recurs. Unless we are prepared to rank societies (or forms of life or cultures), each conflicting claim will be able to display justification as strong as any rival in another society. We have by this route reached no effective adjudication of the claims. The result is a form of fideistic relativism: each society to its own religious and moral truths be true. Thus those who investigated the conflicting claims because they were believers (or unbelievers) felt the most they were entitled to affirm was some form of "they are all true" or "there is some truth in all of them."

Like Bartley and other critical rationalists I find fideism highly unsatisfactory. His diagnosis of the relativist predicament was to trace it to the strategy of adjudicating between claims by seeking their justification, their foundations. It is my contention that the slide towards relativism need never begin were we to break with this strategy and refuse to adjudicate by seeking justification. In the tersest formulation I can manage, a non-justificationist strategy adjudicates between competing claims (not by asking how well each competing view is justified, what foundations it rests upon, but) by asking how criticizable they are and how well criticized they have been.[5]

Bartley set out from the ancient argument[6] that the justificationist project faces an insuperable obstacle: any justifying foundation can be undermined by the simple tactic of asking what it in turn is founded on, what it in turn is justified by. This creates a vicious and unstoppable regress, for any cut-off point is arbitrary. Contemporary relativists favor cutting off the regress at societies, cultures or forms of life. Knowledge claims or standards of value will be founded in and hence justified as a practice of their host society. Questioning the foundations of the society is *ultra vires*. No justification of or beyond social formations is possible; therefore none should be demanded. Unless social formations are self-justifying this cuts off the regress, but in a fideistic way. Later in this essay I shall argue that social formations, beginning with those we belong to, so far from being self-justifying, are open to criticism.

How does the non-justificationist alternative to social and cultural fideism proceed? Suppose one has a criticism of a knowledge claim widely endorsed in a society and wishes to debate its truth or falsity. Should one be stymied by the argument that that is the way people in our society think? Neither in practice nor in theory is this acceptable. In fact, to appeal to one's society or its consensus when one is criticized is to argue from authority. One's society is not a warrant for the correctness, cognitive or moral, of any statement whatsoever.[7] Suppose, in the process of criticism, I make the claim "capital punishment is wrong," and my interlocutor counters with "not always in our society." Our disagreement is only apparent. The claim was not "capital punishment is wrong in your society"; it was "capital punishment is wrong." The first is a putative social fact; the second is a value judgment. If she replies "what do you base that value claim upon?," she makes me an offer that I can and must refuse if I am to avoid being drawn into the justificationist trap. The non-justificationist response is to invite her to criticize the claim that "capital punishment is wrong."[8] For her to observe that her society does not endorse the claim is a criticism of it, but one with little force. If it were as forceful as the relativist implies, we should have great difficulty in being critics and reformers in our society, especially of its consensus or of majority views. Yet in fact we can – and do – conduct debates over the truth of claims, such as "capital punishment is wrong," and understand each other perfectly well and understand just what criticism is being offered when that principle is invoked against a practice.

Admittedly this is somewhat sketchy. Debate over claims, such as "capital punishment is wrong," could take many more forms. It could be asked how consistent the claim was with general rules, such as "killing is wrong" or "crime should be punished." The consequences of the claim could be explained, to see if they are themselves consistent or if they are consistent with other claims. Although in this process of discussion "capital punishment is wrong" has not been justified, it has been critically discussed. Only if it survives many such argumentative challenges could we say it is a claim that deserves to be taken seriously, i.e. further discussed as a putative truth. Its rivals in this and other societies will be assessed by how well they have stood up to such scrutiny. However well they come out, justification is not the result; pointing to alleged foundations is never an answer to criticism.

So much for the outline of my position. Now to develop further the thesis that the plausibility of relativism derives from the justificationist adjudication strategy. Among my illustrations will be that popular and provocative television show *Star Trek – The Next Generation*, which exhibits a fascinating tension between relativist philosophical pronouncements and far-from-relativistic plot resolutions.

But first let me engage in a little more ground-clearing. Three relativisms are conventionally distinguished in anthropology: descriptive, normative and epistemological.[9] To be more precise, these distinctions have been developed as *ad hoc* devices to save the doctrine of cultural relativism (as it was originally and unguardedly put forward) from incoherence.[10] *Descriptive relativism* amounts to little more than the factual and uncontested assertion that societies differ in their cognitive and normative judgments and in the principles by which they make these judgments. *Normative relativism* relativizes all judgments – cognitive, moral and aesthetic – to the

culture (or society) of production. *Epistemological relativism* draws
the conclusion that all pretensions to universal science are without
justification and erroneous to boot: only culturally bound ethnoscience is possible.[11]

In his incisive survey article on "Cultural Relativism and the
Future of Anthropology" of 1986, the cautiously anti-relativist
Melford E. Spiro[12] sums up the underlying claim that normative
relativism makes regarding culture as follows:

> because all standards are culturally constituted, there are no
> available *trans*cultural standards by which different cultures
> might be judged on a scale of merit or worth. Moreover, given
> the fact of cultural variability, there are no universally acceptable
> *pan*cultural standards by which they might be judged on such a
> scale. (p. 260)

To restate that more concretely: "capital punishment is wrong"
cannot be used as a standard to rank different cultures, and cultural variability ensures that we will find some places where that
statement is not accepted as a moral truth. Presumably this is
equally true of cognitive claims, such as "there is no god but Allah
and Muhammad is his prophet."

Optimistic thinkers influenced by the Enlightenment movement
sometimes held that within the observed diversity of societies and
their claims there would be found some agreement and even a progressive convergence[13] as, through the generations, we apply our
universal capacity of reason to the task of ordering society better.
Among the specifics of the capacity to reason was obedience to the
laws of logic. Several putatively transcultural standards are available in logic: take for example the derived rule that an inconsistent
standard is a false standard. The second sentence I quoted from
Spiro presents relativism as the claim that no *pan*cultural standards
are "universally acceptable." This is a very strong formulation. It
could be argued that there are no "universally acceptable" standards even within a culture, never mind panculturally. It is easy to
think of situations where even "murder is wrong" or "cruelty to
children is wrong" would be not uncontroversial and not universally acceptable (e.g. in war, in abortion, in disciplining). Why
should the critic of relativism bother to respond to such an exces-
sive demand as that for pancultural standards that are "universally

acceptable"? Universal acceptability, grounded in the *de facto* consensus, is, I suggest, another justificationist trap.

Focus for a moment longer on the laws of logic: most people in our society know little logic and were its laws stated they would not recognize them, far less assent to them. That hardly tells as an argument against those laws. Universal acceptance, thus, is just too strong a demand. Universal acceptance of, say, material implication with its attendant paradoxes, so-called, can hardly be found even among logicians. The demand for supreme standards and for universal acceptance of them which Spiro is fighting, however, are no mere windmills; they are anti-critical and justificationist. Given that our society is diverse and that it engages in continuous inquiry into logic, into science, into morals and into religion, we can see that the question at hand is not about acceptance, universal or otherwise; the question is "do any of these controversial inquiries make progress?" If they make progress, then that constitutes an answer to relativism, for if we can assess our own efforts then we can also rate those of others and *their* progressiveness. And we must be careful not to repeat the mistake by claiming that the assessment of progressiveness itself will find universal acceptance. Nothing finds universal acceptance, not the roundedness of the earth, not the wickedness of cruelty, not the laws of logic, not the progress of science – not to mention the infallibility of the Pope. Universal acceptance can at most be gained by some authority, Papal or scientific.[14]

THE RELATIVIST CRISIS IN *STAR TREK – THE NEXT GENERATION*

An example of how an enlightened relativism tries to cover up its own authoritarian and justificationist structure is to be found in the syndicated television series *Star Trek – The Next Generation*. The show concerns the voyages of the starship *U.S.S. Enterprise* as it goes about its continuing mission. This is "to explore strange new worlds, to seek out new life and new civilizations, to boldly go where no-one has gone before."[15] Its mission is often described as exploration, that is, observation. Its crew is able to beam in and out of places with matter/energy transfers, able to depart at speeds faster than the speed of light. Various philosophical problems are explored in the show, most notably the boundaries between humans and machines through everyone's favorite character, the android Lt.-Cmdr. Data. In some of the stories the allusion to anthropology gets very near to the surface. (Explorers, travelers (and missionaries) were the forerunners of anthropology.) And where there is anthropology relativism lurks not far way. The location of the crew in an orbiting starship makes them observers rather than participant observers. Indeed, they are like those imaginary ideal observers, the men from Mars.[16]

Inventive script-writers push to the limits of observer-status by constantly placing the starship explorers in positions where the crossover to participation is difficult to avoid. A dilemma is then repeatedly posed. Their exploring operations and orders are governed by a Prime Directive of Star Fleet Command which enjoins that they not interfere with the natural evolution of the new worlds, new life forms and new civilizations which they encounter.[17] Many times this directive is used as a plot point, putting one or more of the *Enterprise* officers into a moral dilemma where their values and instincts need to be explicitly reconciled with the Prime Directive, or else curbed. A complication of other stories brings the Prime Directive into conflict with the captain's primary duty, which is the lives of his crew and the safety of his starship.

Although I appreciate *Star Trek – The Next Generation*, I do not appreciate the Prime Directive – except as a useful way of creating dramatic conflict. First of all, the Directive is explicitly authoritarian, being the supreme order of a military organization, Star Fleet. Second, the Directive smacks of transculturalism rather than what its internal logic suggests, panculturalism: the starship is a product of a specific civilization, the United Federation of Planets. If that civilization is relativist it should seek governing rules for contact that would be widely shared by others. What, then, is the justification from within this culture of the Directive's assertion of a right of all sentient species to evolve normally? Why is quarantining them from the more advanced to be seen as allowing their evolution to be "normal"? The evolution of our own species on this planet involved exploration and contact. We have interacted with many other species. Why should contact with other species, including more developed ones, and its consequent effects, be considered not normal, something to be avoided?[18] Third, it is patronizing: *U.S.S Enterprise* and her officers are the locus of the decision to obey the Directive, whatever the wishes of those they contact, although a nice twist of the plot gives the latter some glimpse of the *Enterprise*'s power and has them try to persuade, trick or blackmail the secrets out of the crew. There is even one episode where the Prime Directive is used as an excuse to erase a child's memory of its visit to the starship before transporting it back whence it came.

Like much relativism, the Prime Directive comes with the best of intentions.[19] Captain Picard's explanation of the reasoning behind the Prime Directive shows that even relativism invites justification. In more than one episode Picard declares that history shows that interference by technologically advanced civilizations with the less advanced invariably led to disaster. Such disasters undermine any attempt to justify interference and the only way to avoid interference is to keep contacts within severe, preferably observer-bound, limits. However, as though aware that relativism is a species of what Walter Kaufmann called "decidophobia,"[20] the writers usually resolve the episode with some sort of compromise.[21] Having tried to avoid interference as much as possible and failed, a responsible decision has to be made even if the Prime Directive is violated.[22] Diplomacy and compromise is Picard's preferred mode and his moral autonomy is enhanced by his ability to take extreme measures – but only responsibly and reluctantly. Compromise of this kind is not relativism.

In an episode entitled "The Masterpiece Society,"[23] the *Enterprise* came across a previously unknown colony of humans who had been isolated in a biosphere on the hostile planet of Moab for 200 years. The colonists had been genetically engineered so that every person was bred to suit some social role, and all disability was bred out. It was clearly though not explicitly a eugenic version of Plato's *Republic*. The biosphere structure was about to be threatened by a close encounter with a core fragment from a neutron star. During the time *Enterprise* was helping avoid this disaster, the chief scientist of the biosphere and some associates decided they would like to leave and see the universe beyond their "paradise." Captain Picard cannot refuse to help people who choose to leave, even though that was not the custom of their country. Yet these departures will interfere with the Masterpiece Society just as much as any technology transfer. Despite the potential damage, the colonists' leader reluctantly authorizes the departures and the unhappy captain comments grimly as the episode ends: "in the end we may have proved just as dangerous to that colony as any [core fragment]" could ever have been.

Yet despite this sort of dramatic self-doubt, the way of life and the science and technology of the starship are taken for granted as the pinnacle of human achievement, all material and medical problems having been overcome. Only self-development remains. The Prime Directive takes the Federation to be superior in a number of ways to some of the life forms with which it comes into contact. Thus it reveals a failure of nerve when it comes to accepting its own superiority. A relativist posture makes the Federation superior only by its own standards and not necessarily by the standards of the other life forms it encounters. If those others dispute the Federation's evolutionary superiority and hence its guardian role, then the Prime Directive can have no primacy. Rather than have the *Enterprise* crew debate rules of engagement with those they contact and opt for the policies that survive criticism, an arbitrary standard (the Federation's own) is imposed.[24] Like all relativism, then, the Prime Directive is internally inconsistent.

The Prime Directive was justified, we recall, by the past history of contact – what history has shown time after time. But there is no inference from past to future, so that is no justification. It was earlier urged that no judgments of fact and value can be justified. At most our claims can be offered as tentative bases for action. Uncritical statements of relativism such as the Prime Directive are self-defeating: they express claims and aspirations while evading the responsibility for decision and choice.

This is apparent in the dramas of *Star Trek – The Next Generation*, where the principle of relativism proves impossible to live by. Much the same is true, I would maintain, in real life. Most people are not relativists in their religion, their morals, their cognitions, or the practices of everyday life. Thus one is suspicious of espousals of relativism and attempts to act it out. There is a famous anecdote about the philosophers Paul Feyerabend and Imre Lakatos when they were waiting for the down elevator in the London School of Economics. Lakatos asked Feyerabend why, since he was a relativist, he bothered to wait for the elevator rather than just jump out of the window and glide down to earth. Feyerabend replied that he would, but only after mastering the technique of flying.

What is the moral of this story? The moral I wish to draw is that, challenged to live his relativism, Feyerabend evaded. As in *Star Trek – The Next Generation*, the values that inspire so much relativism – tolerance, respect for others, appreciation of the different – do not require, and cannot be respected by, trying to fly or practicing voodoo. Toleration, respect for others, appreciation of the different, can be fulfilled by being critical and open minded, aware that compromise requires discussion and ingenuity.

AND AS FOR THE REAL WORLD...

Moving on now from *Star Trek – The Next Generation* to cultural differences in the real world. This essay was delivered at a conference at Wake Forest University, which, in distances calibrated according to the scientific view of the world, is a good way away from where I live. To get to Wake Forest, I boarded an aeroplane built in accordance with that scientific world-view; I did not pray and I did not flap my arms. Being liberal and tolerant, should I have sought a teacher of flying? I think not. In Toronto, where I live, there are some grade schools whose pupils come from more than fifty language-groups, hence cultures, hence diverse backgrounds of cognitive and moral beliefs, and all those children and their parents arrived by aeroplane, and all go for visits to the lands of their ancestors in aeroplanes. They learned about Canada through advanced modern media, and they keep in touch with their relatives and friends by the same means. In doing so they make a pragmatic acknowledgment of the power and superiority of the scientific world-view as it is embodied in the technology of long-distance travel and communications. None flirts with Feyerabend's alternative.

The scientific world-view, however, as Gellner likes to emphasize,[25] cannot easily be restricted to travel and communication: it comes as a package deal. That is, if you see what air travel is all about then (*pace* Feyerabend) you will not from time to time undertake journeys by flapping your arms. The scientific world-view is not an equal rival to such alternative or previous world-views; it supplants them. Furthermore, the scientific world-view embodies and endorses certain standards, including those of truth-telling, progressive change, openness and a critical attitude; underlying these are the basic tenets of logic. Still further, the scientific world-view is universalist and is difficult to reconcile with the remnants of previous world-views that attempt to coexist with it and to somehow partition themselves off from its universalist imperatives. The scientific world-view, in short, is transcultural but not pancultural. It is not justified or founded within any one society or culture, or in any way at all. Its appeal is that it formulates

I. C. Jarvie

persuasive solutions to problems, solutions that are hard to criticize and supersede, yet all comers are welcome to try. This is why it
can and has spread into many societies.

Failure to appreciate this insidious package deal can be illustrated in various ways. One is by the very popularity of *Star Trek –
The Next Generation* itself. Perhaps that is explained because
science can readily be viewed as superior magic. If it can be, then
it is a magic that does not coexist easily with the social institutions
of magical society; it is a cuckoo in the nest. A further illustration
should make this clear. More than twenty-five years ago I made a
study of the Melanesian religious movements known as cargo
cults.[26] These cults erupted on the far-flung islands of the South
Pacific. There appeared to be no possible communication or coor-
dination among the cults. Yet there was a distinct pattern to them.
Prophecy envisaged some kind of upheaval in the world, in which
the social order would be reversed and the precious goods and
cargo which were monopolized by the white man would be delivered instead to the black man. From being powerless the
Melanesians would go to being powerful. They would have all the
material goods they were denied and the millennium would be
ushered in, accompanied by the return of the spirits of the dead.
These beautiful and powerful cult doctrines simultaneously
sought to correct a local problem – the disparity of power, wealth
and material well-being between colonized and colonizers – and
to realize a universal yearning: to see our long-lost loved ones
again. Alas, they appeared to share the presupposition that the
material goods were a product of the colonizer's magic and that
what native Melanesians needed was access to the secrets of this
magic.

Anthropologists labored to produce explanations. There were
Marxist explanations, psychological explanations (mental confusion), symbolic explanations. None of them, however, took the cults
and their ideas completely at face value, namely as explanations of
the Melanesians' predicament, i.e. false explanations that were the
best these societies and traditions could do with events the causes
of which lay totally beyond their experience. Anthropologists and
administrators had been much impressed by the fact that one cult
leader led a cult even after having been taken to Australia for a tour
and shown how the "cargo" goods were made in factories that did
not employ a jot or scintilla of magic.

The world-view of science is universal and comprehensive, but it is very difficult for a society to incorporate it all at once. It is not always clear to what extent traditional views will feel challenged and how that challenge is to be met. From the South Pacific to China, it is noticeable that societies in contact with scientific civilization try to preserve themselves by picking and choosing what to accept.[27] Similarly, on *Star Trek – The Next Generation* the compromise forged by the captain usually minimizes the disruptive effects. In the real world all such compromises are at best partial and temporary. Science and its world-view are restless and probing, never settling down into an assigned niche. Sooner or later any compromise gets upset.[28] The last compromise before accepting the values of science[29] is relativism. I suggest that the relativists in our society are still trying to hedge-in science, to confine its influence. Relativism itself, however, is only a *pro tempore* measure.

Relativism gets adopted because all justifications are equal in their failure. Once we agree to this and assign an equal value to all claims, that value has to be zero. But something must differentiate claims. Science does in the end dominate many debates. If that is not because it is justified, then how comes it? The answer is, I think, straightforward. Science solves the problems and answers the objections better than its rivals. So long as this happens its attraction is not going to wane. If, as I have argued, relativism is defeated by a non-justificationist strategy, and if we take a non-justificationist attitude to the evaluation of cognitive and moral claims, what are the consequences? I wish to wind up the essay by highlighting two consequences among many. The first is that non-justificationism does not require that we treat our own society and its culture of ideas, including religious ideas, as untouchable and due only pious respect; justificationist relativism does. The second is that, on the contrary, a robustly critical attitude is encouraged by non-justificationism, as well as by part, at least, of the intellectual tradition to which we belong. Societies are machines for coordinating the lives of the diverse people who inhabit them, and the changing demands people make on society, as well as the changing environment, ensure that all social machines are in constant need of everything from fine-tuning and tinkering to major repairs or even rebuilding jobs. At times our social machine has incorporated devices we decided were cognitive or moral errors. Among the major *moral* errors that litter the history of our society are chattel slavery, religious wars, cruel and brutal punishment, child labor, animal cruelty, legalized prejudice and discrimination. None of these institutions and traditions has been totally eliminated in any society, yet the record of some, it needs to be said, is better than that of others. What is not warranted, clearly, is any blanket endorsement of our society at any particular point, or of what it has stood for, any uncritical attitude to the machine.

So much is obvious. When deplorable institutions and practices were taken for granted in our society they were elaborately justified in relation to values the society espoused, or, at least, values that large components of the society were said to espouse. Chattel slavery, after all, makes possible, for the slave-owners, a society and way of life different from, and much more physically comfortable than, what is possible without it. Nevertheless, defense of present-day chattel slavery is unconscionable and, in the face of it as a continuing fact, relativist arguments about respect for other cultures, or about the absence of transcultural (or pancultural) standards, is irresponsible humbug. Fortunately, most of those who espouse relativism, like the characters and the writers of *Star Trek – The Next Generation*, are at best well-intentioned but confused, at worst *no more than* humbugs and hypocrites, rather than defenders of slavery.

Prejudice and discrimination are an especially good test of relativism since all known societies practice prejudice and discrimination, both internally and externally. No one here in North America would imagine that our society is free from those things; indeed the very fact that they are often noisily combated or denied is evidence of their persistence. What is a little less palatable is the equal truth that other societies are no better, and in a few cases, worse. Suppose, for example, we were to try to set up a scale to measure religious prejudice, a very difficult task in practice. It is possible that we might find as much or more in other societies, including religious prejudice against us, as in our own. Saddening though the disclosure in our society of any religious prejudice at all would be, can there be any doubt that other societies would show up much higher on the scale?

The relativist would have us take seriously the argument that because the more prejudiced society is a different culture, with different values, its rationalizing arguments are to be taken at face value. They are expressions of "their" culture, and "their" culture is one we must treat with awe and respect because it is different. We, too, should obey some sort of Prime Directive. What no one explains to us is that if we do not take such a tender attitude to our own culture and its past (and present) of religious prejudice and discrimination, why are we obligated to take it towards other cultures? To say it is out of respect for the alien other is highly ethnocentric and inconsistent. It is ethnocentric because other societies, unlike ours, are not shy of judging. It is inconsistent because our society, despite having plentiful prejudice and discrimination, encourages bringing down adverse judgment and thrashing it out. Appeasement is condescending, not respectful.

This yields an interesting result: relativism is less about other cultures than it is an argument within our culture between one side, which elevates certain rarefied and not all that widely held liberal values of anti-prejudice and anti-discrimination into the only correct ones (since they are used to castigate and prevent the expression of the prejudice and discrimination so many of our fellow-members wish to practice), and the other side, which simply wants to do what they have been socialized into doing: act out their prejudices. So relativist liberalism enjoins us to be liberals even towards the anti-liberalism of those we so generously patronize with our liberalism. This is a pretty pickle indeed, and a form of the paradox of toleration.[30]

Our society, and in this we may be more of a template for all societies than we realize, is not unified, not homogeneous. It contains within it disputes about its own policies and outlook. Those who favour robust criticism want disputes articulated, areas of consensus mapped, and the process of debate and compromise begun. Proposals for change are tempered in this process. In the case of religion our society has struggled to become tolerant and secular, not because all religious views are relative but precisely because most religions are absolutist monopolies. Given the presence of multiple and diverse religious groups, toleration and secularism are an agreed way of minimizing the extension of religious conflict to general social conflict. Since no society is homogeneous in religion or anything else, toleration and secularism embody value judgments that emerged from ferocious conflict and have withstood vigorous criticism even though their practical implementation is a site of endless tinkering.

It is only right that we should adopt the same robust attitude to other societies as Captain Picard does in action (as opposed to theory) and, in particular, never take at face value claims of value ("family values") and claims of agreement, consensus ("main-stream") or homogeneity in value, but be as critical of the other as we are of ourselves. Homogeneous societies are imaginary. Every society is a site of struggle, including struggle for the endorsement or relinquishing of values. We are as entitled to our opinions on the material issues raised in an alien society as are the citizens of that society, and we are under no more special obligation to spare the feelings of those acting and speaking in a manner we find egregious than we are at home. (I am ignoring prudential considerations here.) The United States is a foreign land and culture to one raised in Britain and resident in Canada. Does it really occur to any of us not to voice any criticism we have of this country, provided we respect accuracy, civility and responsibility? Why should robust criticism by outsiders upset anyone? If it is true then the society can learn from it; if it is false then it will be discounted.

Canada itself has two founding European nations given to incessant scrutiny and advice-giving, French Canadians and English Canadians. It has quite a few groups of indigenous peoples who are also given to berating the values and practices that have made the white man top dog. I cannot imagine a relativist state of affairs, where Canadians, Americans, Japanese, Québecois, Inuit, and First Nations all simply kept repeating, like a mantra: all cross-cultural judgments are ethnocentric; there are no universally acceptable standards of relative merit or worth; the only normative judgment that can be made is that all cultures and their judgments are of equal worth. This seems to me false and incoherent. False in that no one believes or acts on it for a minute, incoherent because it cannot make sense of the fact that we do articulate transcultural value judgments and have fruitful debates about them.[31]

Notes

1. W. W. Bartley III, *The Retreat to Commitment* (New York: Knopf, 1961).
2. A lot of the negative arguments were drawn together by Richard Rorty in *Philosophy and the Mirror of Nature* (Princeton: Princeton University Press, 1979) in defense of what he called pragmatism but which others have called relativism.
3. It would be an error to assume that social institutions other than language take little or no part in the constitutive machinery of society as a whole, yet some philosophers take that error for obvious fact.

4. There are good reasons for my writing "society" and not "culture," despite current fashion. The theories of sociology and social anthropology explain the bonding of human beings into societies by social institutions and their network of interconnections. No such theory of cultures is available; worse, it is often implied that cultures comprise everything. Yet because the concept of culture is not embedded in any developed theoretical ideas, because it is vague and suggestive rather than clear and precise, its use is conducive to intellectual muddle. This may be precisely why it has become ubiquitous in current debates about the role of language and culture in ethnicity and nationality.

5. Bartley, *The Retreat to Commitment*, op. cit., and *Morality and Religion* (London: Macmillan, 1971).

6. Sextus Empiricus, *Outlines of Pyrrhonism*, I, p. 166; *Against the Logicians*, I, pp. 340–42; *Against the Professors*, II (Rhetoricians), pp. 106–13.

7. This is one of a number of important respects in which the metaphor of games, as in "language-games," is inapposite. (1) The stakes are too high in cognition and morals more than fleetingly to compare one's moves to those of a chess player. (2) Games have and are defined by their rules, rules which are usually written down in authoritative books and, sometimes, governed by international authorities (as in bridge or lawn tennis). These lay down means for settling disputes over the legality of moves. Furthermore, (3) there is a transcendent point of view from which questions external to the game can be asked, such as whether this or that rule should be modified, whether playing this game or any "game" is worthwhile. The language-game metaphor sets philosophy back to pre-Greek times where, G .E. R. Lloyd argues, there was lacking the self-conscious and self-referential consideration of the adequacy of moves or the value of the enterprise. See G. E. R. Lloyd, *Demystifying Mentalities* (Cambridge: Cambridge University Press, 1990).

8. See Popper's British Academy Lecture, "On the Sources of Knowledge and of Ignorance," reprinted in *Objective Knowledge* (Oxford: Clarendon Press, 1972).

9. Most anthropologists are epistemological relativists which, they assume, entails what Philip Quinn calls semantic relativism. Observing five philosophers as diverse as the present company, *none of whom* accepts semantic relativism, must make them classify us as a very odd tribe indeed.

10. Many have tried to pin down these incoherencies; my own efforts are in "Cultural Relativism Again," *Philosophy of the Social Sciences*, vol. 5, 1975, 343–53, and M. Hollis and S. Lukes, eds, *Rationality and Relativism* (London: Routledge, 1984). Karl Popper's are in *The Open Society and Its Enemies* (London: Routledge, 1945 [1962], vol. II, pp. 202–03 and 369–96), and "The Myth of the Framework," in Eugene Freeman, ed., *The Abdication of Philosophy: Philosophy and the Public Good* (La Salle, Illinois: Open Court, 1976). Ernest Gellner's are in "Thought and Time or the Reluctant Relativist" in his *The Devil in Modern Philosophy* (London: Routledge, 1974), chapters 8, 10 and 11 of *Spectacles and Predicaments*

(Cambridge: Cambridge University Press, 1979), chapter 3 of *Relativism and the Social Sciences* (Cambridge: Cambridge University Press, 1985), and "The Uniqueness of Truth," Cambridge: University Printing Service, 1992. See also Harvey Siegel's sustained effort, *Relativism Refuted* (Dordrecht: Reidel, 1987).

11. A clear paradox of self-reference looms here: if the statement "only culturally bound ethnoscience is possible" is within culturally bound ethnoscience, then it is question-begging; if not, it is inconsistent.

12. Melford E. Spiro, "Cultural Relativism and the Future of Anthropology," *Cultural Anthropology*, vol. 1, 1986, pp. 259–86.

13. See Morris Ginsberg, *On the Diversity of Morals* (London: Heinemann, 1956), a book greatly influenced by L. T. Hobhouse.

14. Harvey Siegel, op. cit., pp. 34–8, in his cursory and condescending critique of Popper, says Popper begged the questions because he failed to provide a powerful argument for his nonrelativist stance. He thus berates Popper for refusing to fall into the justificationist trap!

15. In the original series the final phrase was "where no man has gone before." The next generation is more politically correct, yet still splits the infinitive "to boldly go."

16. In fairness to the Webbs, who seem to have been the first to introduce (1932) the imaginary Martian observer, they are clear that what he can observe will only be transient manifestations of social institutions rather than those institutions themselves. See Sidney and Beatrice Webb, *Methods of Social Study*, (Cambridge: Cambridge University Press, 1975), pp. 5–21, esp. 18–19.

17. I have been unable to get an authoritative text of the Prime Directive, but one source gives this:

THE PRIME DIRECTIVE

As the right of each sentient species to live in accordance with its normal cultural evolution is considered sacred, no Star Fleet personnel may interfere with the health and development of alien life and culture. Such interference includes the introduction of superior knowledge, strength, or technology to a world whose society is incapable of handling such advantages wisely. Star Fleet personnel may not violate this Prime Directive, even to save their lives and/or their ship, unless they are acting to right an earlier violation or an accidental contamination of said culture. This directive takes precedence over any and all other considerations, and carries with it the highest moral obligation.

Another source, from the original series of the show, transcribed from the episode, "A Private Little War?", is in the *U.S.S. Enterprise Officer's Manual*, what trekkies call a "noncanon" source:

When contacting a planet making normal progress towards a technological civilization, an officer of Star Fleet shall make no identification of self or mission; no interference with social development of said planet; no references to space, to other worlds or more advanced civilizations."

18. An even deeper problem is whether sentient species can be identified as distinct and separate, and hence separable. This problem is strictly point-of-view relative as regards human societies; it may be naive to think that it is soluble from the point of view of an orbiting spaceship.
19. Gellner writes sarcastically of relativism coming with a halo in "The Uniqueness of Truth," op. cit.
20. Walter Kaufmann, *Without Guilt and Justice: From Decidophobia to Autonomy* (New York: P. J. Wyden, 1973).
21. An example would be the episode, "Who Watches the Watchers?" Some anthropologists hiding on a planet to observe the inhabitants without "contaminating" them accidentally expose their presence. Captain Picard is forced to reveal himself because the inhabitants have taken him for a god. To prevent bloodshed he exposes himself as mortal flesh and blood, but equipped with more advanced technology; he then bids them farewell with encouraging words about the centuries of evolution they have before them.
22. In another episode Picard is formally accused of violating the Prime Directive by a Star Fleet investigator, although it turns out they were querying his record prior to offering a promotion.
23. First broadcast 15 February 1992.
24. An obvious objection is that to debate the rules governing contact involves contact and it is then too late to avoid it, should that be the choice. The alternative is to make all contact situations dominated and controlled by the "superior" contacter. Neither course of action is without its controllable aspects.
25. See also I. C. Jarvie and Joseph Agassi, "A Study in Westernization" (1970), reprinted in Agassi and Jarvie, eds, *Rationality: The Critical View* (Dordrecht: Nijhoff, 1987), pp. 395–421.
26. See the following works of mine: "Theories of Cargo Cults, Parts I and II," *Oceania*, vol. 34, September, December 1983, pp. 1–31 and 108–36; *The Revolution in Anthropology* (London: Routledge, 1964); "On the Explanation of Cargo Cults", *European Journal of Sociology*, vol. 7, pp. 299–312; "Cargo Cults" in *Man, Myth and Magic*, no. 15 (London: British Publishing Corporation), pp. 409–12; "Cargo Cults," *Encyclopedia of Papua and New Guinea* (Melbourne: Melbourne University Press, 1972), vol. I, pp. 133–37. Other literature is cited in those pieces.
27. As in "Chinese learning as the basic structure, Western learning for use," discussed in Joseph Agassi and I. C. Jarvie, "A Study in Westernization," op. cit.
28. Ernest Gellner argues in *Legitimation of Belief* (Cambridge: Cambridge University Press, 1974) that once science is entrenched in a society most of its internal revolutions create nary a ripple in the wider society. Perhaps so. But the process of *introducing* science can be highly destabilizing.
29. I have listed these as truth-telling, progressive change, openness and a critical attitude, and logic. The senior sociologist of science, Robert K. Merton, has an overlapping set: universalism, communism, disinterestedness, and organized skepticism. See his paper "Science and

Technology in a Democratic Order," *Journal of Legal and Political Sociology*, vol. 1, 1942, pp. 115–26, reprinted in various places.
30. See K. R. Popper, *The Open Society and Its Enemies*, op. cit., vol. 1, p. 265.
31. Not all debates, I readily grant, are fruitful. Not all peace negotiations are successful. But philosophers and scientists persist in debating issues that seem bogged down because an impasse does not imply that no breakthrough will ever be found, and most of us agree that most of the time jaw-jaw is preferable to war-war.

5

Will Narrativity Work as Linchpin?
Reflections on the Hermeneutic of Hans Frei

Nicholas Wolterstorff

So that the scripture serves but, like a nose of wax, to be turned and bent, just as may fit the contrary orthodoxies of different societies. For it is these several systems, that to each party are the just standards of truth, and the meaning of the scripture is to be measured only by them.

John Locke, *A Second Vindication of the Reasonableness of Christianity*, in *Works* (12th edition, 1824), vol. 6, p. 295.

When I wrote The Eclipse of Biblical Narrative ... *what I had in mind was the fact that if something didn't seem to fit the world view of the day, then liberals quickly reinterpreted it, or as we say today, "revised" it. And my sense of the matter, though I'm not antiliberal, was that you can revise the text to suit yourself only just so far. There really is an analogy between the Bible and a novel writer who says something like this: I mean what I say whether or not anything took place. I mean what I say. It's as simple as that: the text means what it says.*

Hans Frei, "Response to 'Evangelical Theology: an Evangelical Appraisal'," in *Trinity Journal* 8 NS [1987], pp. 21–2.

A prominent feature of most religious communities in literate societies is the social practice of reading, and in other ways making use of, texts regarded as sacred by the community and

71

treated as canonical. New members of the community *learn* the
practice; they are not born practitioners, nor does mere maturation make them such. And their learning consists of their being
inducted into the practice; the practice confronts them as something already in place – as a *tradition*.

To be inducted into the practice is of course to acquire certain
skills, but it is also to learn of the values which the practitioners
regard as yielded by the practice and to learn how to evaluate both
results of the practice and the manner in which the practice is conducted. Typically, however, these values and modes of evaluation
are contested, both within the community and between members of
the community and those outside; as a consequence, the person
inducted into the practice will typically both be introduced to some
of these controversies and inducted into a particular variant of the
practice.

This, then, is one cause (among others) of the fact that issues of
relativism arise not only *among* religions but *within* particular religions; the problems of understanding and civility posed by the
plurality of religions among human beings in general, and now
within most polities, have their analogues in the problem of understanding and civility posed by the plurality of interpretations and
appropriations of the canonical text *within* religious communities.

My focus in this essay will be on pluralism of this latter, intra-
communal, sort. But I do not wish on this occasion to talk about
such pluralism and the questions of relativism that it raises; I wish
instead to consider how a particular theologian actually dealt with
the plurality of interpretations within his own community. The
Yale theologian Hans Frei in the 1970s and 80s intervened in the
ongoing scripture-reading practice of the Christian community.
That is how his work of those years is to be understood – as an
intervention. Though his project has sometimes been described as
that of developing a theory of biblical interpretation, specifically, of
narrative interpretation, it was not that. Frei regarded most general
theories of interpretation as obstacles to his project; rather than
developing or applying such theories, he typically opposed them.
He acknowledged the existence of a close affinity between certain
of his own assumptions and those of Anglo-American New
Criticism (McConnell, 63–4). But he insisted that his project was not
to take the general theoretical assumptions of New Criticism and
apply them to the special case of the Gospels; it was to intervene in
the Christian practice of scripture-reading, making use of whatever

tools were at hand and useful. His borrowing from New Criticism – if borrowing it was – was purely strategic (McConnell, 72–3).

Frei launched a sweeping critique of a vast number of interpretations of the Gospels offered over the past three hundred years: they ignore, he said, the realistic narrative character of the literal sense of the text. We have a text of the Gospels; it has a literal sense; that literal sense has a realistic character. Furthermore, that character of that sense is accessible "to all reasonable people who know how to relate genus, species, and individual case properly. One appeals first to a qualitatively distinct genus of text (and meaning) called 'literary' and then argues both historically and in principle that within it there is a species called 'realistic narrative' that is quite distinct from, say, romance or heroic epic. To this species, then, biblical narrative is said to belong ..." (McConnell 63). Yet it has become characteristic of the Christian community over the past three hundred years to ignore this character of that sense of this text; there has been an "eclipse of biblical narrative." Frei's response was to mount "a plea" against this eclipse, "on behalf of realistic or literal (as well as figural) reading" (McConnell, 63). And he urged the Christian community to take to heart the lesson he had gleaned, from his own extensive historical inquiry into why the eclipse took place, as to how the practice of interpreting and appropriating scripture must be conducted if the eclipse is to be undone and prevented.

Frei's two books, *The Eclipse of Biblical Narrative* (1974) and *The Identity of Jesus Christ* (1975), are widely regarded as both difficult and obscure. The reputation is not unmerited. It appears to me that some of what Frei saw he never got sharply in focus, and that for much of what he wanted to say, he never found a satisfactory set of concepts. Nonetheless, I think one can discern what he was getting at, and it raises very interesting questions indeed.

I

Near the end of an essay published some time after *The Eclipse of Biblical Narrative* and engagingly titled, "The 'Literal Reading' of Biblical Narrative in the Christian Tradition: Does It Stretch or Will It Break?", Frei remarks that "Established or 'plain' readings are warranted by their agreement with a religious community's rules for reading its sacred text" (McConnell, 68), and he makes clear that, in

saying this, he means to be returning to a point made at the beginning of the essay, in the course of which he said that "the tradition
of the *sensus literalis* is the closest one can come to a consensus
reading of the Bible as the sacred text in the Christian church" (ibid.,
37).

The point Frei is making here requires distinguishing between
what he calls a "plain" or "established" reading (sense) of a text
and what he calls a "literal" reading (sense). Perhaps we can flesh
out his thought along the following lines: there are a number of distinct relations such that if a text stands to an entity of the right sort
in one of those relations, then that entity is a sense of that text.
There is, so Frei and others assume, the *literal-sense* relation: the
relation which holds between an entity of the requisite sort and a
text when the entity is the literal sense of that text. And if we grant
that an author's saying something by way of composing a text
brings it about that what he said is a sense of the text, then also
there is the *authorial-sense* relation. If each of these sense-relations is
such that only one thing can stand to a given text in that relation,
then corresponding to each such sense-relation there will be a function – call it a sense-function – such that, when a text stands to an
entity in that sense-relation, the value of the corresponding sense-
function for that text is just that entity. We can then refer to one
entity as "the literal sense of this text," to another entity as "the
allegorical sense of that text," etc.

In some communities there is sometimes, for at least some of the
texts with which it deals, a "rule for reading," as Frei calls it,
according to which members of the community, when dealing with
a text to which the rule applies, are to focus their interest on just
certain of all those senses which are the values, for that text, of the
various and diverse sense-functions; they are, perhaps, to focus
their interest exclusively on that sense which is the value, for the
text, of the allegorical-sense function. Of course this rule, like all
rules, might be in effect even though some members of the community choose to violate it and dwell on other senses of those texts.
But if in that community at that time there is such a rule in effect
for certain texts, then those senses will be what Frei calls the
"plain" or "established" senses of those texts. For a certain community at a certain time, the established sense of a certain text may be
the literal sense; for a different community or different time or different text, the established sense of the same text may be instead,
say, the allegorical sense.

It is Frei's thesis that in the case of the Christian community the literal sense of its scriptures, especially of the Gospels, has traditionally been the established sense, or at least prominent among the established senses – though Frei thinks that that is no longer the case in the liberal wing of the Christian community.[1] There was no necessity in this, however; in principle, some other sense than the literal might have become established.

> Interpretive traditions of religious communities tend to reach a consensus on certain central texts. We have noted that the literal reading of the gospel stories was the crucial instance of this consensus in the early church. What is striking about this is that the "literal" reading in this fashion became the normative or "plain" reading of the texts. There is no *a priori* reason why the "plain" reading could not have been "spiritual" in contrast to "literal," and certainly the temptation was strong. The identification of the plain with the literal sense was not a logically necessary development, but it did begin with the early Christian community and was perhaps unique to Christianity. The creed, "rule of faith" or "rule of truth" which governed the Gospels' use in the church asserted the primacy of their literal sense. (McConnell, 41)

It should be noted that even if there is a "rule for reading" in effect within a certain community for certain of its texts, and even if all members act in accordance with that rule, it by no means follows that there is consensus in that community on *interpretation* of those texts. When speaking of "interpreting," I shall mean the activity of figuring out in detail the content of that which is the value of some sense-function for a given text – for example, figuring out the content of that which is the literal sense of the text, and when speaking of an "interpretation" I shall mean, correspondingly, the conclusions arrived at by someone's activity of interpreting. An interpretation is a belief or claim concerning the content of some sense.

Thus disputes concerning senses of texts may arise on two quite different levels. There may be disputes over which is the sense-function whose value in a given case we should concern ourselves with – one person may insist that we concentrate on the literal sense of the text, another, that the allegorical sense is more important. But there may also be disputes as to the content of a given sense. Both of these are regularly called disputes over the interpretation. But they take place at different levels, with different considerations being relevant for resolving the dispute. It is of prime importance that we keep the distinction clearly in view.

What is a sense? I have spoken, with total ontological vagueness, of entities which are of the requisite sort to stand to some text in the relation of being a sense of that text. Which sorts of entities are of the requisite sort? Of course, we should not assume unquestioningly that all such entities are of the same ontological category.

The thought which naturally comes first to mind for anyone influenced by Frege is that senses are propositions – *Gedanke*. But it seems to me that such questions as whether at a certain point in a text a writer meant to be asserting something, or meant instead to be asking something, should be construed as questions concerning sense; that difference, however, might not be reflected in any difference of propositions – whatever the answer, it may well be the same proposition which is involved. Accordingly, I suggest that senses are best thought of as sequences of speech actions – where I mean the word "actions" to denote types rather than tokens. Senses are sayings. Frei appears, for the most part, to think of senses instead as propositions; indeed, it is important for part of his argument that they be thought of thus. But that he is not entirely clear on the matter is reflected in the fact that he also sometimes speaks of a sense, or a meaning, of a text as what the text *says*. Sayings, however, are always of some particular illocutionary force; they are never just propositions.

Of course it is not the case that, for a given text, all sequences whatsoever of speech actions are candidates for being a sense of that text; the sequence consisting of asserting that the Soviet Union has broken up followed by asking whether there will now be armed nationalist conflict among the republics can scarcely be a sense of J. M. Coetzee's novel *The Life and Times of Michael K*. Furthermore, a certain sequence of speech actions may have the potential of being a sense of a certain text without actually being that. A full discussion of text and sense would have to address itself to the questions which these points suggest; here I must forswear attempting any such full discussion. I will not attempt to say what, in general, brings it about that a certain sequence of speech actions is a sense of a certain text, nor will I attempt to say how, in general, a sequence of speech actions must be related to a text for the sequence to be capable of being a sense of that text. Perhaps it is worth remarking, however, that sometimes what brings it about that a certain sequence of speech actions is a sense of some text is (in part) that some reader's interaction with the text has taken the form of proposing that sequence as a (or the) sense of the text. Though this action is also frequently called "interpreting" and the result an "interpretation," I shall avoid calling them those things.

The theoretical framework which I have offered in the preceding pages goes well beyond anything to be found in Frei. Nonetheless, there is nothing in what Frei says which leads me to think that he would object to any part of it; it can be thought of as a "rational reconstruction" of his thought.

II

A profound change – so Frei argues – has taken place over the past three hundred years in those practices which the Christian community had developed for reading its sacred scriptures. Frei regularly cites three marks of the change which he has in view: there has been an eclipse of the realistic narrative which is the literal sense of many of these writings; figural (typological) interpretation has fallen into disuse; and no longer do readers fit reality in general into the reality presented by the sacred text but instead fit the sacred text and such reality as they think it presents into reality in general. Let us begin with the first of these, which is the one on which Frei himself places far and away most emphasis.

What does Frei take the literal sense of a text to be? He doesn't say. Presumably he regarded the traditional concept of *sensus literalis* as satisfactory for his purposes. That concept was apparently first used in contexts in which interpreters were claiming that certain texts had senses hidden from ordinary readers, requiring special spiritual faculties or knowledge to discern. These were "spiritual" senses, in contrast to "literal" senses: spirit vs. letter. The term has not shed this part of its history, not in general and certainly not in Frei's usage of it; "literal" is still used to pick out one member of a contrast: literal as opposed to hidden or spiritual – though in using "spiritual" to pick out that which contrasts with literal we will today often be using the word metaphorically. In allegories, one of Frei's favorite examples, there is both a literal sense and a hidden, "spiritual," sense, this latter being the allegorical sense. Vastly more than this could be said about the traditional concept of *sensus literalis* but this will have to suffice. No doubt there will be pairs of contrasting senses such that it is simply unclear which, if either, should be called "literal" and which, if either, should be called "spiritual"; nonetheless I think we can go along with Frei's assumption that the contrast had not entirely lost its utility.

Frei does undertake to explain what he has in mind when he speaks of realistic narrative. (He always credited Erich Auerbach, in *Mimesis*, with being the first to explain the concept of realistic narrative, and with first pointing out that parts of the Gospels satisfy the concept.) When Frei wants one word to describe what he has in mind, the word he always uses is "history-like" – realistic narratives are history-like. He cites three defining features, explaining the first in *Eclipse* as follows:

> By speaking of the narrative shape of these accounts, I suggest that what they are about and how they make sense are functions of the depiction or narrative rendering of the events constituting them – including their being rendered, at least partially, by the device of chronological sequence.... There are, of course, other kinds of stories that merely illustrate something we already know; and there are other stories yet that function in such a way as to express or conjure up an insight or an affective state that is beyond any and all depiction so that stories, though inadequate, are best fitted for the purpose because they are evocations, if not invocations, of a common archetypal consciousness or a common faith. In both of these latter cases the particular rendering is not indispensable, though it may be helpful to the point being made.... (*Eclipse*, 13. Quotations from this work are by permission of the publisher, Yale University Press.)

Frei's thought is something like this: sometimes one's intention in telling a story is such that achieving the intention logically requires telling *this* story and logically requires that one's readers or auditors grasp this story. Let me, as a matter of convenience, say that when that is the case, one's telling of the story is intransitive; otherwise, it is transitive. When a story is told transitively, "the particular rendering is not indispensable," in Frei's words. Of course it is no doubt true that any story whatsoever can be told transitively, but Frei's point seems to be that some stories, by virtue of one and another feature of the story, are inept for transitive telling. Such ineptness is one mark of a realistic narrative.

My explanation of the transitive/intransitive distinction remains somewhat vague in the sense that for a fair number of cases of story-telling it will not be clear whether it is a transitive or an intransitive telling; that is because Frei intended to group together here a number of somewhat disparate phenomena. But I mean the notion of telling a story transitively to cover at least all those cases in which one performs the illocutionary act of telling or writing a story so as thereby to perform some other illocutionary act. By way of telling a story about an ass and some grasshoppers, Aesop said that one man's meat is another man's poison; by way of telling a story about a rich man stealing from a poor man, the prophet Nathan accused King David of criminal behavior; by way of telling a story about a man going on a journey, John Bunyan told another story about the progress of the soul. These are all cases of transitive narration.

The second defining feature of realistic narrative Frei explains in *Eclipse* thus:

> The term realistic I take also to imply that the narrative depiction is of that peculiar sort in which characters of individual persons, in their internal depth or subjectivity as well as in their capacity as doers and sufferers of actions or events, are firmly and significantly set in the context of the external environment, natural but more particularly social. Realistic narrative is that kind in which subject and social setting belong together, and characters and external circumstances fitly render each other. Neither character nor circumstances separately, nor yet their interaction, is a shadow of something else more real or more significant. Nor is the one more important than the other in the story. "What is character but the determination of incident? What is incident but the illustration of character?" asked Henry James. (*Eclipse*, 14–15)

Frei's point here is developed more lucidly in his other book, *The Identity of Jesus Christ*, and more lucidly yet in a long early essay, "Theological Reflections on the Accounts of Jesus' death and Resurrection." Narratives do many things. Perhaps it is plausible, for example, to think of those narratives which are myths as describing states of consciousness. What is characteristic of those narratives which are realistic is that they render the identity of some person or some character. We feel that we come to know, through the narrative, who that person is, his "singular unsubstitutable identity" as Frei is fond of calling it – provided, of course, that we regard the narrative as accurate. In the case of novels, we feel that the character is "brought to life."

There is, however, a variety of ways of trying to communicate who someone really is, the choice one makes depending in part on one's views concerning identity; if one thinks of human beings as fundamentally self-reflexive centers of consciousness, or as creatures in search of an identity which they lack, then one will not use realistic narrative to render their identity. It is characteristic of realistic narrative, as Frei understands that, to make use of two "patterns" for rendering identity; Frei calls them the intention-action pattern and the subject-manifestation pattern. His discussion persuades me that the second is not really a pattern of description but a condition which a narration of a person's intentions and actions must satisfy if that narration is to present us with the identity of the person (or the character).

The intention-action pattern of description is this: in realistic narrative one tells who someone is by presenting a sequence of his intentional actions and undergoings, this including those about which one wants to say that "Here he was most of all himself." We come to know who he is from those actions, on the assumption that

> who a person is, is first of all given in the development of a consistent set of intentions embodied in corporeal and social activity within the public world in which one functions. When a person's intentions and actions are most nearly conformed to each other – and further when an intention-action combination in which he plays a part is not merely peripheral to him but is of crucial importance, involving his full power in a task – then a person gains his identity. A person's identity is constituted (not simply illustrated) by that intention which he carries into action. ("Theological Reflections", p. 279)

The subject-manifestation condition is this: if such a sequence is indeed to tell us who someone is, it must give us more than what is characteristic of the person at the moment and more than what is characteristic of his public persona. It must tell us who the abiding self behind the persona is. For that, the narrative must satisfy this condition: that the sequence of the person's intentional doings and undergoings manifest (express) the true abiding self of the person. The assumption is that "behind" the actions there is a "subject who is the same in himself and in his manifestations. Neither is he a static substance accidentally connected with what is externally manifested of him so that he does not himself appear in it, nor is he an identity distortedly manifest so that he does indeed appear in his manifestation but only in alienation or *Entäusserung*" (ibid., 286).

In summary, "the inextricable, mutual involvement of specific, unsubstitutable chains of events with equally specific individuals is a common feature of historical description and the narrative of the classical novel" (ibid., 263).

The third defining feature is explained in the following:

> realistic narrative, if it is really seriously undertaken and not merely a pleasurable or hortatory exercise, is a sort in which in style as well as content in the setting forth of didactic material, and in the depiction of characters and action, the sublime or at least serious effect mingles inextricably with the quality of what is casual, random, ordinary, and everyday. The intercourse and destinies of ordinary and credible individuals rather than stylized or mythical hero figures, flawed or otherwise, are rendered in realistic narratives. Furthermore, they are usually rendered in ordinary language .... Style and account go together.... Believable individuals and their credible destinies are rendered in ordinary language and through concatenations of ordinary events which cumulatively constitute the serious, sublime, and even tragic impact of powerful historical forces. (*Eclipse*, 14–15)

Indispensable to understanding Frei's subsequent argument is the recognition that the history-likeness of the literal sense of some text implies nothing whatsoever as to the truth or falsity of the propositional content of that sense. From the history-likeness of the literal sense of some work of history one can conclude nothing whatsoever as to its accuracy; from the history-likeness of the literal sense of some work of fiction one can conclude nothing whatsoever as to how closely it was modeled, if at all, on real-life persons and places and events. It is true, says Frei, that readers living before that revolution in interpretation whose history he wishes to trace assumed without question that history-likeness reflects historicity: "the realistic feature had naturally been identified with the literal sense which in turn was automatically identical with reference to historical truth" (*Eclipse*, 11); "if it seemed clear that a biblical story was to be read literally, it followed automatically that it referred to and described actual historical occurrences" (ibid., 2). But in fact the literal sense of a text may be a realistic narrative without the story, the narrative, having occurred.

It is tempting to think of Frei in this discussion as having delineated for us a certain literary genre – the genre of realistic narrative. But that would be a mistake. Realistic narrative, as understood by Auerbach and Frei, does not constitute a genre – in the sense in which "genre" is used by literary critics. For genres are literary types handed down in a tradition as forms which writers can try to exemplify in their compositions; the literary type sonnet is an example. But there isn't any literary type realistic narrative which was handed down in a tradition to first-century gospel writers, to nineteenth-century French novelists, and to twentieth-century American historians, which they can all try to exemplify in their compositions. Whatever literary type the gospel writers were trying to exemplify, if any, it was not this. Though realistic narrative does indeed constitute a (more- or less-delineated) type, it does not constitute a genre; works of different genres belong to the type.

The other two features of traditional interpretation which the changes of the past three hundred years have served to eclipse can be dealt with more briefly. There has been an eclipse of figural or typological, interpretation, in which one entity or event is construed as the "type" of another, this other then being the "antitype" – King David being a type of Christ, for example. Frei regularly insists that typological interpretation is not a species of allegorical interpretation; in typological interpretation, attention remains focused on the realistic narrative which is the (propositional content of the) literal sense. "Far from being in conflict with the literal sense of biblical stories," he says, "figuration or typology was a natural extension of literal interpretation" (*Eclipse*, 2). I think he is right about that – provided we construe "natural," in "natural extension," as meaning not unnatural.

The sense of a narrative, on the account I have suggested, is a sequence of sayings – of speech actions. In the case of the authorial sense of a work of history, those sayings will be, for the most part, assertions: the historian asserts that such-and-such happened or was the case. In the case of the authorial sense of a work of fiction, those sayings are (on my view) for the most part invitations to imagine; the fictioneer invites us to imagine such-and-such. Though a few of the sayings, that is, the speech actions which comprise the senses of texts, do not have propositional content – for example, such sayings as "Hi" and "Ouch" and "Oh" and "Whee" – for the most part they do have propositional content; they are assertings, askings, commandings, wishings, requestings, invitings to imagine, etc. Now a concept which has proved of great utility in understanding our interaction with texts is the concept of *the world* of a work – or, strictly, the concept of the world of a work with respect to a sense. The world of a work (with respect to a sense) is more expansive than the propositional content of that sense. For in reading we always extrapolate beyond what is actually said – even beyond what is said and verbally suggested. And the world of a work (with respect to a sense) is to be thought of as what is said and verbally suggested plus what is appropriately extrapolated from that. To arrive at the world of the work (with respect to a sense) we have to flesh out, in appropriate ways, what is said and verbally suggested.[2]

The great majority of the principles that we in the modern world make use of for this fleshing out are principles of logic and causality. If the twenty-first birthday of some character is described for us, we extrapolate to his having had a twentieth birthday, even though it is neither said nor verbally suggested that he did. If in a work of contemporary history we are told that someone got from Edinburgh to London in less than two hours, we extrapolate to his having made the trip by plane.

Figural or typological interpretation is a mode of extrapolation. Suppose one's vision of historical reality is such that one not only regards entities as standing in causal relations to each other but also as standing in relations of signification: this historical thing, person or event signifies that one. Then in all likelihood if one is concentrating on the literal sense of some text, and that literal sense is "history-like," one will not only extrapolate from the propositional content of what is said and verbally suggested by appealing to one's causal convictions; one will also do so by appealing to one's convictions as to the signification relations which hold among historical entities. Such extrapolation is figural, or typological, interpretation. Let me in fact henceforth call it extrapolation, so as to keep before us its fundamental difference from what I have been calling interpretation (i.e., figuring out what is contained in some sense). Auerbach explains figural extrapolation very well, in a passage quoted by Frei:

Figural interpretation establishes a connection between two events or persons in such a way that the first signifies not only itself but also the second, while the second involves or fulfills the first. The two poles of a figure are separated in time, but both, being real events or persons, are within temporality. They are both contained in the flowing stream which is historical life, and only the comprehension, the *intellectus spiritualis*, of their inter-dependence is a spiritual act.

In this conception, an occurrence on earth signifies not only itself but at the same time another, which it predicts or confirms, without prejudice to the power of its concrete reality here and now. The connection between occurrences is not regarded as primarily a chronological or causal development but as a oneness within the divine plan, of which all occurrences are parts and reflections. (Quoted by Frei in *Eclipse*, 28–9)

Frei's thesis, then, is that as those realistic narratives which are the literal sense of so much of scripture were eclipsed from view, typological extrapolation likewise fell into disuse, since typological extrapolation *just is* extrapolation from (the propositional content of) those literal senses which are history-like narratives. Of course, it might have fallen into disuse in any case – I do not read Frei as denying that. Typological extrapolation falls into disuse if people no longer think of items in history as bearing signification relations to each other.

And thirdly, before the revolution in interpretation took place, "the direction in the flow of intratextual interpretation [was] that of absorbing the extratextual universe into the text, rather than the reverse (extratextual) direction" (McConnell, 72). The "direction was that of incorporating extra-biblical thought, experience, and reality into the one real world detailed and made accessible by the biblical story – not the reverse" (*Eclipse*, 3). Again Frei cites a passage from Auerbach, one in which Auerbach is contrasting Homer's *Odyssey* with Old Testament narrative:

Far from seeking, like Homer, merely to make us forget our own reality for a few hours, it seeks to overcome our reality: we are to fit our own life into its world, feel ourselves to be elements in its structure of universal history .... Everything else that happens in the world can only be conceived as an element in this sequence;

into it everything that is known about the world ... must be fitted as an ingredient of the divine plan. (Quoted in ibid.)

Now, says Frei, it is different. Readers of the scriptures try to fit that text and its world into reality in general – understanding this as they have been instructed to understand it by secular scientists and historians.

III

It is by no means Frei's contention that the narrative of the literal sense of the Gospels is realistic throughout. He sees the gospel narratives as having three parts. The first part consists of the pre-birth, birth, and infancy stories; here there is very little realistic narrative. In this part, the character "Jesus" "is not the individual person, Jesus.... He is not even an individual Israelite, but Israel under the representative form of an infant king figure. He is a representative person in barely individuated form" (ibid., 293). The second part, from the baptism up to the passion, shows definite traces of realistic narrative. Yet the emphasis is on the message of the Kingdom of God; "it is perhaps precarious to make the claim," says Frei, "but it does seem that at this stage he is identified by the kingdom, rather than the kingdom by him" (ibid., 294). It is in the passion and resurrection sequence that the narrative becomes fully realist; now Jesus "is simply himself in his circumstances, truly a person in his own right" (ibid., 295). Now the story's focus

remains on Jesus as the unsubstitutable person he is in his own right through passion as well as resurrection.... In both [passion and resurrection], he is equally himself, none other than Jesus of Nazareth. In the unity of this particular transition, passion to resurrection, he is most of all himself.... The difference is that whereas in passion and death this identity is *enacted* in the particular circumstances in which he is most of all himself, in the resurrection his identity is presented to us as that same one now ambiguously and rightly *manifested* as who he is.... In the resurrection he is most nearly himself as a person who is an individual in his own right. He above all others is totally at one between manifestation and the identity manifested. (Ibid., 296–7)[3]

In that last dark sentence, Frei is alluding to his conviction that the character "Jesus" is delineated in the culmination of the Gospels as one whose identity *requires* that he rise from the dead. His resurrection is essential to his presented identity, in the sense that for someone to exhibit the "Jesus" character of the Gospels, that person would not only have to have the property of rising from the dead if killed; this would have to be one of his essential properties. So, at least, I construe what Frei has in mind when, speaking of the climax of the story, he says that "what the accounts are saying, in effect, is that the being and identity of Jesus in the resurrection are such that his nonresurrection becomes inconceivable" (*Identity*, 145). "[D]isbelief in the resurrection of Jesus is rationally impossible" (ibid., 151); "to conceive of him as not living is to misunderstand who he is" (ibid., 149); "to think him dead is the equivalent of not thinking of him at all" (ibid., 148). Frei concedes that "it may be dubious wisdom to make Luke or John speak like a late eleventh-century theologian." Nonetheless he goes on to say that "something like this argument seems to me to be present in the resurrection account" ("Theological Reflections," 299). Sometimes, at least, Frei sees that this contention about the character "Jesus" may be true, while the question remains open as to whether the historical Jesus, or anyone else, ever had this property essentially; for he adds that "one could presumably still see this as a literary feature or part of the description of the account, and therefore either leave the factual question suspended or answer it separately in the negative" (ibid., 299).

A question arises as to how Frei's claim that the Gospels are narrative renderings of the identity of Jesus is to be fitted together with his claim that these narratives, as they move from infancy to resurrection, change in character from being hardly at all realistic to being intensely so. I find Frei unclear on the matter. One possibility is that he regarded only the third part of the gospel narratives as rendering the identity of Jesus; the other parts do something else. I think it more likely that he thought of the Gospels in their entirety as rendering the identity of Jesus, with only the third part of each doing so in realistic fashion. This third part, however, is the controlling part. The other parts are to be read in the light of this part: the parables are the parables told by the one who was raised after being crucified.

IV

Frei takes it as obvious that scripture reading as practiced by Christians has changed over the past three hundred years in the ways indicated; he spends no time assembling evidence. His energy is focused on unearthing the cause of the change.

Though he hints now and then at other factors, Frei's emphasis falls overwhelmingly on an assumption concerning realistic narrative – mistaken in his view – which he sees pervading the period in question: the assumption that meaning is reference, as he regularly puts it. "The explicative meaning of the narrative texts came to be [seen as] their ostensive or ideal reference" (Eclipse, 124).

It is by no means clear what Frei means by "meaning is reference" – what assumption he attributes to his predecessors. I think the most plausible surmise is that it is the assumption that, for realistic narratives, the meaning of the sentences is facts which the sentences pick out. If one thinks one has gotten hold of the meaning, but that proves not to be a fact, then one hasn't gotten hold of it. Frei's own view is that the meaning is the sense, rather than any reference; realistic narratives "mean what they say."[4]

Frei appears to have regarded this assumption, all by itself, as accounting for some of the obliviousness to those realistic narratives which are the literal senses of the Gospels. Rather than using the various literary-critical techniques which Frei himself thought appropriate to illuminating realistic narrative, a person who held this assumption would be inclined to dispense with those, rush right past the literal sense, and concern himself with those historical facts which are, supposedly, the sole meaning of the narrative. Historical interests would displace literary.

Quite clearly it was Frei's conviction, however, that what gave this assumption its real power was the presence of two other factors in the situation. For one thing, those who were Christians were extremely reluctant to draw the conclusion that the Gospels lack meaning; perhaps a sentence here and there, but no more than that. And, secondly, there was skepticism concerning more and more passages in the Gospels as to whether what at first blush appeared to be the literal meaning of those passages really did pick out facts. Given the assumption that meaning is reference, one could take this skepticism in either of three directions: one could

88   *Nicholas Wolterstorff*

conclude that the literal meaning must be something other than what at first appears to be the literal meaning, since that is not factual. Or one could hold that this is indeed the literal meaning, but insist that, since it is not factual, the literal meaning cannot be the real meaning; it cannot be the meaning which is of concern to Christians. Or one could conclude that the passage does not have a literal meaning since there is no other plausible candidate for that, but this one cannot be that since it is not factual. The first of these options would not yield oblivion to the literal meaning of the Gospels and its history-like character, but only in isolated instances would it be reasonable to pick this option.

So it was that this trio of factors caused oblivion to those realistic narratives which are the literal senses of the Gospels – and a whirling search for meanings other than the realistically narrative literal. Here is how Frei himself makes the point in one passage:

> Meaning and narrative shape bear significantly on each other. Even if one was convinced that the history-like or realistic character of the narratives finally bespoke an illusion, so that their true history either had to be reconstructed historically or their true sense explained as allegory or myth, the realistic character was still there. This led to the odd situation described above. Some commentators explained the realistic feature by claiming that the stories are reliably or unreliably reported history. Others insisted that they are not, or only incidentally, history and that their real meaning is unconnected with historical reporting. In either case, history or else allegory or myth, the *meaning* of the stories was finally something different from the stories or depictions themselves, despite the fact that this is contrary to the character of a realistic story. (*Eclipse*, 11)

Frei sometimes formulates the crucial mistaken assumption a bit differently: the history-likeness of the literal sense of the Gospels was assumed to be identical with its historicity. The force of this is no different, however, from the meaning is reference doctrine when that is applied to realistic narrative. The thought is that the history-like narrative, which is the (propositional) content of the literal sense, was identified with some stretch of history, i.e. with some historical facts:

commentators, especially those influenced by historical criticism, virtually to a man failed to understand what they had seen when they had recognized the realistic character of biblical narratives, because every time they acknowledged it they thought this was identical with affirming not only the history-likeness but also a degree of historical likelihood of the stories. Those who wanted to affirm their historical factuality used the realistic character or history-likeness as evidence in favor of this claim, while those who denied the factuality also finally denied that the history-likeness was a cutting feature – thus in effect denying that they had seen what they had seen because (once again) they thought history-likeness identical with at least potentially true history. (*Eclipse*, 11–12)

Is it true that the changes in practice which Frei details were due to the "unhappy inability" of interpreters over the past three centuries "to make some appropriate logical distinctions" (*Eclipse*, 136) between meaning and reference when confronted with realistic narratives? I very much doubt it. What first plants a question in my mind is the fact that, though Frei quotes liberally from a great many interpreters over the past three centuries, none of them in any of the citations offered comes anywhere near saying that meaning is reference. By itself, that is not an objection to Frei's thesis: they might have been taking meaning to be reference without ever saying so. The claim that they were doing that would just be Frei's way of conceptualizing and describing their practice; it might fit their practice without any one of them ever having conceptualized and described his or her practice in that way.

What makes it almost certain, however, that they were not doing that is that this way of thinking and proceeding has an obvious implication which is obviously absurd. If meaning in general were reference – as Frei understands that – there would be no meaningful falsehoods. If the meaning of a sentence were some fact that the sentence picks out, then perforce a sentence that failed to pick out a fact would lack meaning. But sentences which express falsehoods do fail to pick out facts. So if history-likeness were historicity, history books would contain true sentences and meaningless sentences but nothing in between – no meaningful sentences expressing falsehoods. Now it just might be that an individual thinker here and there, when dealing with realistic narrative, operated with an understanding of the meaning of such texts which has this preposterous consequence, but it passes credulity to suppose that a large number of highly intelligent thinkers over three centuries would operate with any such understanding. And in fact – to cite just one writer whom Frei mentions – John Locke certainly did not. Locke explicitly thought of sentences as expressing propositions, and divided propositions into the true and the false.

My own suggestion is that the eclipse of which Frei takes note was the consequence of two dynamics quite different from the one Frei emphasizes, dynamics produced by alterations of practice and of conviction rather than by confusions about meaning. The first was an alteration in the practice of interpreting the canonical texts which took place among certain groups in the seventeenth century and came to clear and explicit expression in the writings of John Locke. For Locke the core of revealed, as opposed to natural, religion was episodes in which God reveals something to someone. It was Locke's view that one is never entitled to believe immediately that God has revealed something to so-and-so. One is entitled to do so only on evidence, and it was his view that only miracles provide the requisite good evidence. It was furthermore his view that, though testimony concerning purported miracles and concerning purported episodes of revelation is, in principle, acceptable as a basis for believing that they have occurred, such testimony is never to be believed immediately but is always to be evaluated for its reliability. Locke applied these views to his reading of the Gospels by regarding them as the testimony of ancient men concerning purported episodes of revelation and purported confirmatory miracles – combined, indeed, with the expression of a good deal of natural human wisdom – and by assuming that that testimony is to be accepted only after being evaluated for reliability.

What Locke takes for granted, without ever to the best of my knowledge arguing the point, is that the reading and interpreting of scripture is not itself a mode of revelation; the classic Protestant teaching that, by way of one's proper and receptive interpretation of scripture, God now speaks to one has no place in Locke's thought. The Gospels are, at most, reliable records and reports of ancient episodes of revelation – not instruments of present revelation.

I submit that someone who reads the Gospels in this fashion will be unconcerned with the narrative structure of their literal sense. Interest will be displaced from structure of narrative to incidents of ancient history. The text and its narrative are of merely instrumental interest for the evidence they provide as to what happened in those times. Close interpretation of the narrative of the literal sense of the text is religiously irrelevant.

There was a second dynamic, to some extent interacting with the first; let me call it the pressures of canonicity, or better, new pressures of canonicity. Frei alludes to this dynamic without ever giving it prominence in his account. Here is one such allusion:

> The specter now barely visible on the horizon was that important, indeed hitherto central portions of the Bible, no matter if they made referential sense did not make abiding religious or moral sense at all, so that they are in effect really obsolete.... What appeared ... was the suspicion that the accounts mean what they say, but that what they say is not only an untrue or unverifiable but is an insignificant claim as well.... To explicate them properly is to erect a formidable barrier to any possible applicative sense. That was the impossible option which no thinker across the religious spectrum would have countenanced then or, for that matter, today. (*Eclipse*, 133)

About the dynamic of which he here takes note, Frei asks the question: "Why should the possibility be ruled out that this is indeed the meaning of the texts, and that it may well be religiously anachronistic or at least without direct religious consequence for anyone today?" (ibid., 132) His answer seems to me off-target: it was ruled out, he says, because of "the apologetic urge," "for which explication and application had to walk in harmony"; this, then, is "one reason for the strange eclipse of the realistic narrative option" (ibid., 134). I suggest that the dynamic on which Frei has his eye here is not the apologetic urge but the pressures of canonicity in a situation of burgeoning historical skepticism.

Consider some religious community which has certain texts which it regards as canonical. Suppose there is widespread agreement in the community on the benefits desired from the use of those canonical texts, in particular, from the interpreting of them; the community enjoys near consensus on what might be called canonical benefits. It is characteristic of religious communities to want and expect of their canonical texts that they will provide access to a certain domain of truth and serve the cause of religious edification. Suppose, secondly, that senses of those texts have gotten established in the community (in the sense of "established sense" explained earlier). Suppose, thirdly, that there is an established practice of interpreting those senses which yields results (i.e., interpretations) on which there is widespread agreement;[5] the practice may yield fresh interpretations in the hands of some practitioners, but when it does, consensus emerges about their cogency. Suppose, fourthly, that there is also an established practice of appropriating those interpretations which yields results, i.e. applications, on which there is widespread agreement. (This too is not to be viewed as incompatible with novelty of results.) And suppose, lastly, that there is widespread agreement that those appropriation-practices of those interpretations of those senses yield desired and expected canonical benefits.

Now suppose that someone, whether a member of the community or not, presents an argument to the effect that, contrary to what members of the community had supposed, the outcome of the chain moving from text to sense to interpretation to application does not possess or yield the canonical benefits which the community desires and expects from that chain. Perhaps he argues that the propositional content of one of the standard interpretations which plays a key role in the community's appropriation is false. One option for the community is to reject the conclusion of the argument. But if it accepts the conclusion, then perforce it has introduced cognitive dissonance into its life and some revision is called for if equilibrium is to be restored.

One option, abstractly speaking, is for the community in some way or other to alter the canon so as to remove the offense. Someone might propose, for example, that the Letter of James be deleted from the Christian canon, or that a different, non-offending version of the text which has caused the problems be adopted. There are not many significant issues for which adopting a non-offending variant of the text proves to be a live option, and proposals to slice whole chunks out of the canon never gain consensus. Ordinarily the person who argues for deleting texts from the canon is deleted from the community!

Another option for the community is to alter its views concerning canonical benefits. The community has always supposed, let us say, that this text properly interpreted and properly applied will not only yield access to certain fundamental truths about God but also to certain truths about the origins of the cosmos. The tension may be resolved if the community changes its mind about the latter desired and expected benefit and no longer uses the text to find out about cosmic origins, resting content with using it to find out about God. It is obvious that religious communities do change their expectations concerning the benefits of appropriating their canonical texts, often under exactly the sorts of pressures suggested.

But sometimes, depending on the character of the original objection, the alterations required for relieving the pressure by changing expectations concerning canonical benefits would be so radical that other options look more attractive: release that sense from being the established sense, or alter the practice of interpreting that sense so that a different interpretation acquires consensus, or alter the practice of appropriation so that a different application acquires consensus.

I submit that the changes in practice to which Frei calls attention have been caused, in great measure, by the pressures of canonicity in a situation of rising skepticism as to the truth of more and more parts of the (propositional content of the) literal sense of the Gospels. Some part of the content of the literal sense seemed false to an interpreter; yet, as a member of the Christian community, he was willing neither to propose discarding this text from the canon nor to propose that the community drop its demand for true interpretations which are edifying in their application. Hence the interpreter proposed an alternative sense, or an alternative interpretation of the literal sense, or an alternative application of the interpretation. In so far as the first was the option taken – and Frei details how often it was – biblical narrative was eclipsed.

V

Frei's suggestion as to how to prevent the eclipse of biblical narrative follows straightforwardly from his analysis of its cause. The suggestion comes in two parts. First, keep sharply in mind that meaning is not reference. What this implies for practice is that issues as to the truth or falsity of the literal sense of the narrative are not to intrude into one's interpretation. Only *after* one has finished interpreting is one to ask whether the propositional content of one's interpretation is true. Frei speaks in the counterfactual mood in the following passage, but the thought is very much his own:

in order to recognize the realistic narrative feature as a significant element in its own right ... one would have had to distinguish sharply between literal sense and historical reference. And then one would have had to allow the literal sense to stand as the meaning, even if one believed that the story does not refer historically....

In both affirmative and negative cases, the confusion of history-likeness (literal meaning) and history (ostensive reference), and the hermeneutical reduction of the former to an aspect of the latter meant that one lacked the distinctive category and the appropriate interpretive procedure for understanding what one had actually recognized: the high significance of the literal, narrative shape of the stories for their meaning. (*Eclipse*, 11–12)

Let us be clear on what this means: it means interpreting the Gospels so as to make no commitment even to the existence of a person named "Jesus" – reading them simply as the delineation of a *character* "Jesus." Whether the historical Jesus exhibited this character, whether he more or less did so, whether the writers of the Gospels thought he did, whether anyone at all has exhibited this "Jesus"-character – these, on Frei's view, are questions to be postponed until interpretation is finished.

The Gospels:

tell a story of salvation, an inalienable ingredient of which is the rendering of Jesus as Messiah, and ... whether or not he was so in historical fact, or thought of himself as Messiah (i.e. whether the story refers or not), or whether the notion of a Messiah is still a meaningful notion, are different questions altogether. To the "narrative" perspective, these latter questions would have to do not with meaning or hermeneutics but with an entirely separable historical and theological judgment. Hermeneutically, it may well be the most natural thing to say that what these accounts are about is the story of Jesus the Messiah, even if there was no such person; or, if there was, he was not in fact the Messiah; and quite regardless of whether or not he (if he did exist) thought of himself as such.... (*Eclipse*, 133–4)

Second, borrow from literary critics whatever strategies seem appropriate for illuminating the realistic narrative character of the literal sense of the Gospels, and use them in the conviction that "it

is not going too far to say that the story is the meaning or, alternatively, that the meaning emerges from the story form, rather than
merely being illustrated by it.... If one uses the metaphorical
expression 'location of meaning,' one would want to say that the
location of meaning in narrative of the realistic sort is the text, the
narrative structure or sequence itself" (*Eclipse*, 280).

Frei had high expectations for the consensus on interpretation
which this approach would yield. In a thus-far unpublished lecture
which he delivered at Harvard in 1967, entitled "Remarks in
Connection with a Theological Proposal," he remarked that "my
plea here is – the more formal, the less loaded we can make the
notion of understanding, the better. And that, in turn, involves a
search, in deliberate opposition to most of what I find in contemporary theology, for categories of understanding detached from the
perspectives we bring to our understanding, including our commitments of faith."[6] He then went on to say that "my proposal ... is
that in regard to aesthetic or quasi-aesthetic texts, particularly narratives – and the Gospels are such in part – 'normative' interpretation may be possible. That is to say, the meaning of the text remains
the same, no matter what the perspective of succeeding generations
of interpreters may be. In other words, the constancy of meaning of
the text is the text and not the similarity of its *effect* on the life-
perspectives of succeeding generations."[7]

Unfortunately for Frei's hopes, though non-constancy of
meaning would indeed tend to yield a corresponding non-
constancy of interpretation, constancy of meaning is no guarantee
whatsoever of constancy in the interpretations of that meaning. Not
only do we bring our divergent perspectives to our judgments
about the truth of narratives; we bring them to our interpretations
of the narratives.

VI

Frei's intervention was a significant stimulus to the tremendous
flowering of interest in biblical narrative which has occurred over
the past decade or so. But rather than halting with a celebration of
this fact, let us press on and ask why Frei thinks it so important
that the Christian community not neglect the realistic narrative of
the literal sense of the Gospels. Sometimes in Frei, and rather often
in his followers, one gets the impression that the *thereness* of the

realistically narrative literal sense is regarded as sufficient reason
for attending to it – indeed, sufficient reason for its being prominent among the senses established in the Christian community. But
surely there might, abstractly speaking, be good reasons for continuing to neglect this sense. Immanuel Kant, for example, was of the
view that though it may once have been worthwhile for the
Christian community to attend to the literal sense of the Gospels,
the maturation of the community toward increasing rationality
implies that that is no longer the case; Kant proposed an alternative
sense.

We enter here the murkiest part of Frei's argument. It would be
an imperceptive reader indeed who did not interpret *Eclipse* as a
plea for the recovery, at least in the Christian community, of attention to the realistic narrative sense of the Gospels; indeed, Frei
himself, as we have seen, speaks of his proposal as "a plea on
behalf of realistic or literal (as well as figural) reading" (McConnell,
63). Yet when finally it comes to the point that we need an argument for the importance of the literal sense, not just for its thereness, Frei begs off – or gives the impression of begging off. He says,
for example, that his essay "The 'Literal Reading' of Biblical
Narrative in the Christian Tradition: Does It Stretch or Will It
Break?" is not "an argument on behalf of [the] continued viability"
of establishing the literal sense. And then he adds: "that viability, if
any, will follow excellently from the actual, fruitful use religious
people continue to make of it in ways that enhance their own and
other people's lives, without the obscurantist features so often and
unhappily associated with it" (McConnell, 37). Along the same
lines, later in the same essay he asks:

> What of the future of the "literal reading"? The less entangled in
> theory and the more firmly rooted not in a narrative (literary) tra-
> dition but in its primary and original context, a religious commu-
> nity's "rule" for faithful reading, the more clearly it is likely to
> come into view, and the stronger as well as more flexible and
> supple it is likely to look. From that perspective, a theory
> confined to describing how and in what specific kind of context a
> certain kind of reading functions is an improvement over the
> kind of theoretical endeavor that tries to justify its very possibil-
> ity in general. (McConnell 61–2)

But perhaps we should not interpret Frei in these passages as saying that he intends to be purely descriptive; that is, perhaps we should not interpret him as repudiating the aim of intervening in the ongoing practice by Christians of reading and interpreting their canonical scriptures. Perhaps we should instead interpret him in these passages as indicating how he proposes to ground his plea – and how, in his judgement, such a plea should be grounded. It should not be grounded in "theories of hermeneutics," nor in arguments for the historicity of the content of the Gospels (McConnell, 62). It should be grounded in the religious utility, for the community, of making the literal sense, with its realistic narrative character, the established sense. If one wants the community to change its practice, one must persuade it of the religious utility of so doing.

I judge this to be how Frei was in fact thinking. Yet he is remarkably chary of stating what he thinks that religious utility to be. He does offer some hints, though; so let me assemble those. *Eclipse* can be read as a plea for pure narrativism: what counts is just the story. That proves not at all to be Frei's view.

All that he has said so far, says Frei, "is right in the marrow of the story. As a literary account, the gospel story makes Jesus accessible to us. The question is, does it open up the possibility of a more than literary accessibility of Jesus to us? If so, at what point? Where could one make the transition from literary description to historical and faith judgments?" ("Theological Reflections," 290)

His thesis has been, says Frei, that the crucifixion–resurrection sequence of the Gospels concerning Jesus is "(1) where the bond between intention and action in his story is most clearly evident; and (2) where the direct bond between himself as individual subject and his outward self-manifestation is strongest and most clearly unitary in character" (ibid., 263). "The obvious implication of this claim is that if one is to make the mysterious and always problematical transition from literary description to judgments both of historical fact and of faith concerning this particular story and its significance, it is at this climatic point of Jesus' resurrection that one must do so" (ibid., 264). If the transition is to be made at all, it should be made at that point where the individuality of the character "is most sharply asserted and etched" (ibid., 298).

Not only is the question of factuality allowed at that point; it is invited, even forced. Why is that? In one passage Frei says that "the

passion-resurrection account *forces* the question concerning its factuality" because "what the authors are in effect saying ... is that the
being and identity of Jesus in the resurrection are such that his nonresurrection is inconceivable" (ibid., 298–9). But here Frei's
Anselmian language has led him into confusion. Suppose someone
writes a novel, clearly labeled thus, in which a character is delineated of a sort such that a person could exhibit that character only if
one of the person's essential properties was that of being resurrected if killed. I submit that none of us would raise the question of
factuality at that point in our reading of the novel; we would
instead just think of the novel as ingenious.

In another passage Frei, in almost glancing fashion, suggests an
answer to his question which seems to be more on target: "if a
novel-like account is about a person who is rightly or wrongly
assumed to have lived, *the question of factuality is bound to arise precisely at the point where his individuality is most sharply asserted and
etched*" (ibid., 298; cf. *Eclipse*, 140). What invites or forces one to
raise the question of factuality concerning those points of a narrative where a character's individuality is sharply etched is one's
belief that the narrative is asserted – that it is offered as a description of an actual person. Stories *qua* stories, no matter how realistic,
do not invite the question of factuality – certainly not in our novel-
laden societies. Rather, given a story of the sort Frei specifies, it is
one's belief that the story has been presented as (in part, at least) a
true description of someone that encourages or impells one to raise
the question whether some specific person, or some person or
other, exhibited the character delineated. One can see why Frei is
reluctant to make this point, however: the belief that someone
offered a story as truly rendering the identity of some person is a
belief that so-and-so took place in history!

To find oneself impelled to raise the question whether the historical Jesus exhibited the character "Jesus" in respect to its most
sharply individuated aspects is not, however, to find oneself
impelled to answer "Yes" to the question. The truth is that whereas
some people find themselves believing that the story presents the
identity of the historical Jesus,[8] some do not. The difference of
response is inexplicable, says Frei; "why some believe and others
do not is impossible for the Christian to explain" (*Identity*, 152).

Frei appears to recognize that such believing-on-say-so is a case
of immediate, as opposed to inferential, belief: "no matter what the
[internal] logic of the Christian faith, actual belief in the

resurrection is a matter of faith and not of arguments from possibility or evidence" (*Eclipse*, 152). And quite clearly he recognizes that,
in tacitly assuming that such immediate belief is (sometimes at
least) entitled, he is bumping up against an epistemological tradition which affirms the contrary: "I am well aware of, but not terri-
bly distressed by, the fact that my refusal to speak speculatively or
evidentially about the resurrection of Christ, while nevertheless
affirming it as an indispensable Christian claim, may involve me in
some difficult logical tangles" (*Eclipse*, xiii). He also recognizes that
such immediate believing-on-say-so would not be entitled under
all circumstances: "reliable historical evidence *against* the resurrection would tend to falsify it decisively, and ... the forthcoming of
such evidence is conceivable" ("Theological Reflections," p. 302).
Presumably evidence that Jesus did everything possible to elude
his captors and evade execution – that his behavior was far from
"obedient" – would also remove entitlement.

Frei makes one additional epistemological point in this connection, namely, that we have no better access to the identity of Jesus
than through the gospel narratives: "if what is said to have happened here is true, there is no evidence in its favor other than that
which we have already adduced" (*Eclipse*, 151). "[I]n the Gospels,
which tell us most of what we know about Jesus, his identity is
grasped only by means of the story told about him" (ibid., 87). In
particular, though "the endeavor has frequently been undertaken,
there appears to be no independent historical or other evidence that
leads strong or conclusive support to the likelihood that this event
[of the resurrection] took place or that it belongs to a credible type
of occurrence.... There appears to be no argument from factual evidence or rational possibility to smooth the transition from literary
to faith judgment" (ibid., 151). The fact that evidence is lacking is in
part coincidental; in part, however, it lies in the nature of the case:
"both because what is said to have happened here is, if true,
beyond possible verification (in this sense unlike other 'facts'),[9] and
because the accounts we have and could most likely expect to have
in testimony to it are more nearly like novels than like history
writing, there is no historical evidence that counts in favor of the
claim that Jesus was resurrected" ("Theological Reflections," 302).

In short, though Frei no doubt regarded attention to the literal
sense of the Gospels as beneficial to the Christian community for a
number of reasons, all of his attention was focused on just one
reason: he assumed the importance to the community of access to

the identity of Jesus Christ, and he urged that "it is precisely the fiction-like quality of the whole narrative, from upper room to resurrection appearances, that serves to bring the identity of Jesus sharply before us and to make him accessible to us" (*Eclipse*, 145).[10] His argumentation, mainly hermeneutical, partly epistemological, partly practical in its reference to canonical benefit, was in defense of that conviction.

VII

There is much indeed that is worth discussing about Frei's intervention. Here I shall have to limit myself severely to a few comments about the structure of the intervention.

Frei's conclusion as to the root of what had gone wrong over the past three hundred years in the Christian practice of interpreting the Gospels was that interpreters required of their interpretations that they be true and edifying, with the result that the thereness of the realistic narrative of the literal sense of the gospel texts was eventually lost from view. The text became a wax nose, interpreted as one wished. In the face of this rampant pluralism of interpretations, Frei tirelessly insisted that interpreting be insulated from appropriating. First interpret, then appropriate. Do not allow your views as to the truth or falsehood, utility or inutility, of a proposed interpretation to play a role in your decision whether to accept or reject that as an interpretation of the text. Protect interpreting from the pressures of canonicity.

But when we press the question why Frei thinks the realistic narrative so important, the larger picture that emerges looks very different. The linchpin of Frei's argument is his conviction that the canonical benefit of gaining access to the identity of Jesus Christ is of fundamental importance to the Christian community; he assumes, without comment, that not much else about the historical Jesus is of fundamental importance to the community. The argument itself is that this benefit can be achieved by combining a certain practice of interpretation with a certain practice of appropriation. The practice of interpretation is that of interpreting the literal sense of the Gospels in a literary way. The practice of appropriation is that of making the transition from story to history at the point in the Gospels where the identity of Jesus is most sharply displayed, namely, in the passion–resurrection sequence, the transition itself consisting of believing on the say-so of the gospel writers that Jesus of Nazareth had the identity that the character "Jesus" was delineated at that point in the Gospels as having. To those whose epistemology implies that this transition is impermissible, sanctioning, as it does, believing certain things immediately on say-so which the epistemology implies are permissibly believed only on evidence, Frei says that their epistemology is mistaken.

In this larger picture, considerations of truth and utility, so far from being set off to the side, are at the very center. Frei's call for interpreting the literal sense of the Gospels in literary fashion is grounded on his claim that epistemologically responsible access to the truth about the identity of Jesus Christ can be gained, and can only be gained, by taking the results of such interpreting and appropriating them in the manner he recommends.

And let it be noted that the truth in question is, in part at least, a truth of history. The historicity of the gospel narratives proves no less important to Frei than it was to large numbers of his predecessors; the narrative of the Gospels yields access to history. But it yields epistemologically responsible access only to a very narrow slice of history – namely, to the identity of Jesus of Nazareth, who is the risen present Lord. Frei's underlying contention is that the community should both treasure and be content with that narrow slice. Whereas his predecessors (as Frei interprets them) saw historicity linked to history-likeness by *meaning*, Frei sees them linked (in the Christian community) by *faith*. It may be added that the traditional view that proper reading of the scriptures is a mode of revelation in the present (and was a mode of revelation in the past) is as absent from Frei's line of thought as it was from Locke's; that this is "the Word of God" does not function in his argument.[11]

Though my casting things in this light amounts to a criticism of Frei's way of presenting his intervention, it is not a criticism of the structure of the intervention itself; every significant intervention will exhibit a similar structure. Current practices of using canonical scriptures are said to yield undesired results, or not to yield desired results; a proposal is then made for revising the practices of interpreting and/or appropriating so that the undesired results are prevented and the desired ones secured. Equilibrium is thus restored. But always of course the restoration requires revision at some point or other; the challenge is to reflect on the options until it becomes clear which is the best way of restoring equilibrium.

Nicholas Wolterstorff

The undesired result which Frei constantly cites is that biblical narrative has been eclipsed. But when we ask what is wrong with that, something much more basic for Frei comes into view: the current practices eclipse the identity of Jesus Christ – except, perhaps, for the practices of those on the "right" who operate in pre-critical fashion, not acknowledging the consensus of historical-critical scholars that very little can be said with confidence about the life of Jesus. Frei, let us remember, assumes that that consensus is well-grounded; he does not contest it. Though he sometimes speaks as though his aim was to recover pre-critical practices, he at most proposes recovering pre-critical practices of interpreting; pre-critical practices of appropriating are to be drastically revised. He asserts that part of "the *minimal* agreement about reading the Scriptures" in the Christian community has been that "Christian reading of Christian Scriptures must not deny the literal ascription to Jesus ... of those occurrences, teachings, personal qualities and religious attributes associated with him in the stories in which he plays a part ... "(McConnell, 68–9). But it turns out that his allegiance to that "minimal agreement" is subtle and highly qualified.

Fundamental evaluation by the Christian community of Frei's intervention will have to address itself to assessing the importance of the canonical benefit which lies at the basis of his proposal – and that done, to determining whether the practices he proposes are likely to yield that benefit (without foreclosing on others which severally or jointly may be of even greater moment). And it must by no means be supposed that everyone in that community would agree with Frei on the importance he assigns to access to the identity of Jesus Christ. Those on the "right" would say that the community can and must gain access to much more of Jesus than his identity, those on the "left" that either such access is not likely to be secured, or the benefit of securing it is of less importance than other benefits which can be secured.

But what, lastly, about Frei's contention that to achieve the truth and utility of access to the identity of Jesus we must not permit our judgments as to the propositional content of the literal sense of the Gospels to be influenced by our views as to the truth or falsehood, utility or inutility, of that content? Just exegete the story! Three or four points are worth making.

It would be impossible to accept, as a general policy, that one not allow one's convictions as to the truth or falsity of the propositional content of proposed interpretations to influence one's judgment as to the acceptability of the interpretation. This is most clear in the case of metaphors; to get at the literal sense of the text, as Frei understands that, we have to decide which words are being used literally and which metaphorically. In very many (though not all) cases of metaphorical use, what persuades us that we are in the presence of metaphor is our conviction that the words taken literally yield a falsehood which the writer would have recognized as such and, on that ground, not wished to assert.

Second, Frei's claim that we are to interpret realistic fiction and history in the same way, the difference (for the reader) turning up only at the point of appropriation, will not do. The issue turns on whether a sense should be thought of as a sequence of speech actions or as a sequence of propositions. I have argued for thinking of it in the former way. Though Frei is ambivalent on the matter, he often thinks of it in the latter way. He holds that we should interpret the sense of a realistically narrative text in a way neutral as between history and fiction because it is neutral as between history and fiction. Only *after* one has discerned the propositions constituting the sense should one inquire into the extra-sense phenomenon of mode of presentation – fictive, assertive, etc. The fact that the gospel texts are presented as claims, as "testimony," is an extra-sense, historical fact about them and should be allowed to enter the picture only after interpreting is finished. My own view, as I have indicated, is that part of what goes into the skilled exegesis of works of fiction is discerning where, amidst the fictionalizing, assertions are being made, wishes expressed, etc. Frei himself, as we have seen, rather often speaks of the meaning of a text as what it says. But sayings have illocutionary force as well as (in most cases) propositional content.

In part our disagreement here is verbal: will we count speech actions as part of the sense or not? In part it raises issues much too large to consider here concerning the nature of texts and how they acquire senses. But one consequence of cutting the pie in Frei's way, which he wouldn't at all like, is that conclusions as to the content of the sense of a text can only be made *after* conclusions have been drawn about the (supposedly) extra-sense fact of mode of presentation. That is the case because if, for example, I make claims about some actual person Jesus, I am expressing different propositions from any that I would be expressing if I were just telling a story in which I delineate a character "Jesus." If I am making claims about some person Jesus, then I am referring to him and predicating something of him, and the proposition I express is true if and only if *he* exists and has the property I predicated of him. The proposition is a singular one. But if I am only telling a story in which I delineate a character "Jesus," I am not expressing that proposition nor (on my view) any other singular proposition. It is true that many texts are such that they might be (or have been) composed either as fiction or description; maybe that is true in general of realistic narrative. But the propositions expressed will not be the same. If we cut the pie in Frei's way, extra-sense phenomena contribute to determining sense. (Of course it would be open to Frei to respond by saying that the fact that by composing the text its writer or editor asserted such-and-such a proposition does not establish that that proposition belongs to its sense.)

A final comment: the picture one gets from Frei is that only in the modern period have interpreters within the Christian community allowed the pressures of canonicity to shape the interpretations they offer. But in fact this is as old as the Christian community itself. Though the members of the ancient church were extremely open-minded about the occurrence of "wonders" in history, they had very firm views about the nature of God. They believed that since God enjoys perfect being, God is a-pathetic. Accordingly, when they came across passages of scripture in which the apparent literal sense was the ascription to God of emotions, they concluded that the apparent literal sense could not be the real literal sense, for they were not willing to concede that their scriptures might not be accurate in speaking about God. A lot of what makes scriptural interpretation in the modern world different from what it was in the ancient world is that we more readily concede that God suffers than that God works "wonders."[12]

Notes

1. In those writings of his which preceded the McConnell essay, Frei often spoke of texts, and in particular, of realistic narrative texts, as just having a meaning or as just saying something. The McConnell essay, in recognizing that texts in general may have several meanings, one or more of which may be established, is more sophisticated. I shall formulate Frei's thought in terms of the McConnell essay, even though that sometimes requires recasting what he actually said, and sometimes even requires discarding what he said. For example, in his

earlier writings Frei often claims, concerning realistic narratives, that they just "mean what they say." This claim must be allowed to fall by the way, since it falsely assumes that such texts have just one sense and that their meaning is *that sense.*

2. The concept of the world of a work is elaborately developed in my *Works and Worlds of Art* (Oxford: Oxford University Press, 1980).

3. Cf. Frei in "Response," 22: "I cannot take the biblical story, the gospel story especially, in separation from its being the identification, the literal identification of someone identified as Jesus of Nazareth. It's not about something else, not about somebody else. And it's not about nobody in particular, nor is it a story or an allegory about a mode-of-being in the world or something of that sort, although it may include that kind of dimension."

4. I have not tried, and will not try, to explain what Frei means by "meaning."

5. This may be the consequence, in part, of there being a "rule of faith" in accord with which that sense of those texts is interpreted. See Frei, in McConnell, 41–2, and George Lindbeck, "Scripture, Consensus, and Community" in R. J. Neuhaus (ed.), *Biblical Interpretation in Crisis* (Grand Rapids: Eerdmans, 1989), p. 75.

6. Quoted in George Hunsinger, "Hans Frei as Theologian: The Quest for Generous Orthodoxy" in *Modern Theology* (vol. 8, no. 2, April 1992), p. 109.

7. Ibid. Cf. this passage from *Identity*, xv: "The aim of an exegesis which simply looks for the sense of a story (but does not identify sense with religious significance for the reader) is in the final analysis that of reading the story itself. We ask if we agree on what we find there, and we discover its patterns to one another. And therefore the theoretical devices we use to make our reading more alert, appropriate, and intelligent ought to be designed to leave the story itself as unencumbered as possible. This is additionally true because realistic stories, perhaps unlike some other texts ... are directly accessible. As I have noted, they mean what they say, and that fact enables them to render depictively to the reader their own public world, which is the world he needs to understand them, even if he decides that it is not his own real world.

8. And they, accordingly, use the story to refer. Says Frei: "That does not mean that I don't believe that we refer by *means* of that story. We do refer by means of that story and I would say that we refer in a double sense. There is often a historical reference ..." ("Response," 22). Frei's thought appears to be that although the story's literal sense is devoid of reference, persons can *use it* to refer. Perhaps the original writers used it thus; we can do so as well. But whether it is or is not so used, the story means what it says; it does not mean what it is used to refer to.

9. And that, in turn, is so in part because Jesus is the eternal Word made flesh: "Is Jesus Christ ... a 'fact' like other historical facts? Should I really say that the eternal Word made flesh, i.e., made fact indeed, is a fact like any other? I can talk about 'Jesus' that way, but can I talk

about the eternal Word made flesh in that way? I don't think so, just as I don't think that I can say 'God created the world' and mean by that a factual referent like any other" ("Response ," 24). Perhaps the deepest source of the difference between Locke's approach and Frei's is Locke's Socinianism in contrast with Frei's Calcedonian Trinitarianism.

10. Cf. Frei in "Response," 22–3: "We start from the text: that is the language pattern, the meaning-and-reference pattern to which we are bound, and which is sufficient for us. We cannot and do not need to 'transcend' it into 'limit' language and 'limit' experience.... The truth to which we refer we cannot state apart from the biblical language which we employ to do so. And belief in the divine authority of Scripture is for me simply that we do not need more. The narrative description is adequate. 'God was in Christ reconciling the world to himself' is an adequate statement for what we refer to, though we cannot say univocally how we refer to it."

11. Though it is an element in his theology. Cf. "Response," 22: "We do refer by means of that story and I would say that we refer in a double sense. There is often a historical reference and often there is textual reference; i.e., the text is witness to the Word of God, whether it is historical or not. And when I say witness to the Word of God, I'm not at all sure that I can make the distinction between 'witness' to the Word of God, and Word of God written."

12. Cf. the following interesting passage from Leibniz (*New Essays on Human Understanding*, tr. & ed. by Peter Remnant and Jonathan Bennett [Cambridge: Cambridge University Press, 1981], 499–500): "But it seems to me that a question remains which the authors I have just mentioned did not investigate thoroughly enough, namely: suppose that on the one hand we have the literal sense of a text from Holy Scripture and that on the other we have a strong appearance of a logical impossibility or at least a recognized physical impossibility; then is it more reasonable to give up the literal sense or to give up the philosophical principle? There are certainly passages where there is no objection to abandoning the literal sense – for instance, where Scripture gives God hands, or attributes to him anger, repentance and other human affects. Otherwise we would have to side with the Anthropomorphites, or with certain English fanatics who believed that when Jesus called Herod a fox he was actually turned into one. This is where the rules of interpretation come into play; but if they provide nothing which goes against the literal sense in deference to the philosophical maxim, and if furthermore the literal sense contains nothing imputing some imperfection to God or involving a threat to pious observances, it is safer and indeed more reasonable to keep to the letter."

References

Frei, Hans W., *The Eclipse of Biblical Narrative: A Study in Eighteenth and Nineteenth Century Hermeneutics* (New Haven: Yale University Press, 1974). Abbreviated as *Eclipse.*

Frei, Hans W., *The Identity of Jesus Christ: The Hermeneutical Bases of Dogmatic Theology* (Philadelphia: Fortress Press, 1975). Abbreviated as *Identity.*

Frei, Hans W., "The 'Literal Reading' of Biblical Narrative in the Christian Tradition: Does It Stretch or Will It Break?" in Frank McConnell, ed., *The Bible and the Narrative Tradition* (New York: Oxford University Press, 1986). Abbreviated as McConnell.

Frei, Hans W., "Response to 'Narrative Theology: An Evangelical Appraisal'," in *Trinity Journal* 8 NS (1987). Abbreviated as "Response."

Frei, Hans W., "Theological Reflections on the Accounts of Jesus' Death and Resurrection" in *Christian Scholar* 49 (1966). Abbreviated as "Theological Reflections."

Concluding Responses

Comments

Philip L. Quinn

I would like to organize my response to the essays of my colleagues, Professors Hollis, Jarvie, Phillips and Wolterstorff, around a distinction between two forms of relativism. Epistemic relativism involves the relativization of epistemic statuses such as being justified or being rational. Semantic or metaphysical relativism involves the relativization of reference or truth or both. There are individualistic forms of both doctrines, but it is more common to find groups, for example, societies or cultures, spoken of as the things to which other things are relative. Moreover relativism can be global, extending to beliefs of all sorts, or local, covering only the beliefs in a certain domain such as morality or religion.

Epistemic and semantic relativism are, of course, not the only varieties of relativism of interest to philosophers. Thus, for example, though the relativism espoused by Runzo that I criticize in my paper is a version of semantic relativism, it has its roots in a doctrine of conceptual relativism. I restrict my focus to epistemic and semantic relativism for tactical purposes. My colleagues and I all use the term "relativism," but it is not obvious that we are all addressing the same issue or small set of issues. Given the diversity of our backgrounds and interests, this should come as no surprise. Nevertheless, I shall argue that my colleagues all do have things to say that bear on questions of epistemic or semantic relativism. I shall also try to spell out some of the implications of these things for religious belief.

With respect to the domain of religion, local epistemic relativism is a plausible and now widely held view. Certain Christians are justified and quite rational in believing that ultimate reality is personal, i.e. God. But certain advaitic Hindus are equally justified and rational in believing that ultimate reality is impersonal, i.e. Brahman. In both instances, having taken account of both experience and testimony and having given a fair hearing to objections to their views, these believers remain within their epistemic rights, so to speak, in having the religious beliefs they do. However, absent further assumptions, epistemic relativism does not imply or entail semantic relativism. So it seems that one can consistently endorse epistemic relativism about religious beliefs while insisting that either the beliefs of the Christians or the beliefs of the Hindus or both are false. Since justified false belief is a common enough phenomenon, an argument will be required to persuade us to make the transition from epistemic relativism to semantic relativism in the religious domain.

I take it that Ian Jarvie's essay is best read as addressing the issue of epistemic relativism. One reason for thus construing it is that it associates relativism with what he regards as a flawed epistemological position, which he calls "justificationism" but others would call "foundationalism." According to justificationism, justified beliefs must have proper foundations or grounding in social practice, experience, rational intuition, authoritative texts or the like. The alternative to this position Jarvie plumps for is familiar; it is Popperian critical rationalism. What is not clear is whether critical rationalism can do much to help in overcoming epistemic relativism in the religious domain.

I grant that the method of conjectures and refutations helps in the formation of worldwide rational consensus in communities of expert inquirers in mathematics and natural science. But I doubt that it has anything like the same power when it comes to matters of morals and religion. To be sure, we can expect widespread agreement about a few things, though perhaps Jarvie's example of wanton cruelty being wrong[1] is unfortunate because it involves an analytic truth. After all, if there were acts of cruelty that were not wrong, we would not describe them as wanton. Still, few would dissent from the view that Hitler was an extraordinarily vicious man. And, similarly, most would agree that Jim Jones did not happen upon the true salvific path in Jonestown. That, however, leaves plenty of room for rational disagreement in both morality and religion.

Of course I concur with Jarvie in thinking there is no impropriety involved in articulating cross-cultural value judgments and criticizing moral and religious views with which we disagree. But should we expect such criticism to be rationally compelling, that is, to persuade those with whom we disagree that their views are mistaken or irrational? Very often, I submit, we should expect no such thing. Consider, for instance, the quarrel between the tradition of moral inquiry that favors a virtue ethics of Aristotelian or Thomistic provenance and the tradition that endorses a deontological ethics of a Kantian kind. Each tradition criticizes the other and responds to criticism by the other, but neither has been shown by the criticism of the other that it currently confronts problems which, by its own lights, it ought to be able to solve but lacks the resources to solve. The adherents of each tradition are within their epistemic rights in having the moral beliefs presently characteristic of that tradition; those beliefs are rational and fully justified. And there is no realistic prospect that, in the foreseeable future, further applications of the techniques of critical rationalism will alter matters in the direction of convergence on a single consensus about rational or justified moral beliefs. Rational disagreement is highly likely to persist for a very long time over large areas of the landscape of the moral domain.[2]

I expect the persistence of rational disagreement in religion as well, particularly among the so-called "world religions"; they have, after all, evolved over millennia very complex and sophisticated intellectual defenses or systems of negative apologetics. So I am willing to bet that epistemic relativism will remain true to some extent within the realm of religious belief far into the future, perhaps interminably. I am therefore very skeptical about whether critical rationalism can do much, if anything, to change this situation.

There is in D. Z. Phillips's paper an interesting argument for a certain sort of semantic relativism in the religious realm. As Phillips notes, it stands in the tradition of Feuerbach's reduction of theology to anthropology. Its conclusion is that "religion is relative to the cultural context in which it flourishes, and that God has no existence independent of it." This conclusion invites us to suppose that God is no more than a cultural construct, an internal object of human culture. God exists in some but not all cultures. Hence the term "God" succeeds in referring in some cultures but fails to refer in others, and so the belief that God exists is true in some cultures and not true in others.

On the face of it, this claim is quite implausible and would be completely unconvincing if we were asked to accept it simply on the basis of its intrinsic obviousness or self-evidence. There is, however, an argument for it to be found in Phillips's paper, and that argument deserves consideration on its own merits. In my opinion, it is unsound because among its premises is the erroneous assumption that the term "God" is not a name.

As it is typically used in theistic discourse, the term "God" may indeed not be a proper name in some of the technical senses now current in analytic philosophy of language. Contemporary philosophy of language furnishes the resources to formulate a whole host of fascinating questions about the usage of the word "God" in theistic language-games. Is it a title and therefore equivalent to some Russellian definite description? Does it express what Searle thinks of as a cluster-concept? Is it a Kripkean rigid designator? Does a causal theory of reference apply to it so that it refers to whatever entity the ancient Israelites baptized when, say, Moses encountered it? All these are very interesting technical questions. But however they may be answered, one thing seems abundantly clear. In the usage of the vast majority of traditional theists, the term "God" functions as a referring expression of some sort, and the object to which theists mean to refer by using it transcends all human cultures. Thus, far from being relatively innocent descriptive observations about the grammar of the term "God," the remarks Phillips makes on this topic are, and ought to be recognized as, deeply radical proposals for revision in traditional theistic linguistic practices.

Curiously enough, Phillips himself challenges the validity of this argument for semantic relativism. Though he seems to accept the assumption that the term "God" is not a name, he denies that it entails the relativistic conclusion that God dies with the demise of certain cultural practices. "No such conclusion follows," he says, "since the language of faith allows the believer to speak of such an eventuality." He supposes the believer would say that the world had turned its back on God in such an eventuality. But if the believer is mistaken in thinking that the term "God" refers to something that transcends all human cultures, the believer is also mistaken in thinking or saying that God would survive the demise of certain cultural practices. So even though Phillips is probably right about what the believer would say, this does not suffice to show that the argument for semantic relativism under consideration in his paper is invalid.

It is of course possible, for all I know at any rate, that Christianity may cease to exist. I am persuaded that it is a central tenet of Christian faith that this will not in fact happen. Being omnipotent, God has the power to prevent it from happening. Being perfectly good and having promised that it will not happen, God will do what he can to keep his promise and so will succeed in bringing it about that it does not happen. If, nevertheless, Christianity were to cease to exist, what would the upshot be? Not, I think, the death of God, as if the existence of God, like the existence of the intentional objects of our fantasies and dreams, depends on us or our activities.

From the point of view of the Christian tradition, this would be an idolatrous supposition, substituting some human creation for the transcendent creator of heaven and earth. Rather, the upshot would be the sad loss of many true beliefs about ultimate reality, beliefs that are non-relativistically true and not just true for Christians or in Christendom. It is therefore clear that the mere possibility of Christianity becoming a museum-piece by itself does little, if anything, to support semantic relativism in the religious domain.

I must say that Nicholas Wolterstorff's account of Hans Frei's project gives me a better sense of what Frei was trying to accomplish than I had ever gotten from my own reading of Frei. What remains a bit unclear, however, is how Frei's work bears on issues of relativism in the religious domain. So let me suggest one way in which materials adapted from Frei's thought might be used in the construction of an argument for a kind of semantic relativism.

Frei points out a difference between the literary genre of realistic narrative, which is defined by being history-like, and the historical truth or factuality of narratives in the genre. Thus, for example, both Leo Tolstoy's *War and Peace* and Barbara Tuchman's *The Guns of August* belong to the genre, but the former is much less factual than the latter. Much of what Scripture tells us about Jesus, particularly about his passion, death and resurrection, takes the form of realistic narrative, but there is no consensus among biblical scholars about how much of this narrative is factual. What implications does this have for Christian faith?

One answer to this question involves a rather facile relativism. The Christian community is supposed to derive canonical benefits from appropriating the scriptural narrative and somehow interpreting the world so that it fits into the narrative's structures and categories. Imagine that the community could obtain those benefits even though the narrative was almost entirely devoid of factuality. On a pragmatic conception of truth according to which the true is identified with the beneficial, the narrative would be true for the community despite its lack of factuality. And, of course, other realistic narratives, equally lacking in factuality, would be true in this sense for other religious communities if they were to yield the appropriate canonical benefits to those communities.

This is not Frei's answer to the question. Though he concedes that the gospel narratives are not factual on all points of detail, he considers it essential to a proper Christian appropriation of their story of Jesus that factuality be claimed for that portion of the

narrative, its passion–resurrection segment, which reveals the identity of the character of Jesus in the story. According to Christian
faith, the historical Jesus has the identity of the character of Jesus in
the story, and so what reveals that identity in the story, preemi-
nently its passion-resurrection episode, must also be true, factually
and non-relatively, of the historical Jesus. All this is an echo of the
familiar idea that Christians are a miserable people whose faith is
vain if Christ be not risen. However, I confess that this idea seems
correct to me. Like Frei, then, I would insist on the importance to
Christian faith of claiming non-relative factual truth for much of
the gospel narrative and of rejecting relative pragmatic truth as not
good enough. I would therefore resist the attempt to deploy Frei's
work in support of semantic relativism. This seems easy to do
because the pragmatic conception of truth employed in mounting
the argument for relativism is particularly crude. After all, even if it
is granted that patriotic emotions are on the whole beneficial, we
would not want to say that *War and Peace* is true for the Russians
but not for the French because reading it with care tends to evoke
such emotions in the Russians but not in the French.

Martin Hollis's paper discusses arguments for semantic relativism
that try to show that reality is in some sense internal to such things
as language games, conceptual schemes or theories. He acknowledges the Kantian truism that percepts without concepts are blind
and, hence, that there is theory all the way down in our beliefs. But
then, following Robin Horton, he makes a distinction between
primary and secondary theory. Primary theory deals with middle-
sized perceptible objects. Apparently a single primary theory is universally shared, or almost so. Most of the beliefs that belong to it are
non-relatively true, and so it offers no foothold to semantic relativism. By contrast, secondary theories differ strikingly from one
community to another, and their objects are hidden or unobservable. Secondary theories function to explain disturbing or anom-
alous events or phenomena, and presumably epistemic relativism
holds at the level of secondary theory. Hence there might be a sound
argument from epistemic relativism to semantic relativism within
the domain of secondary theory. Since primary theory underdeter-
mines secondary theory, it seems plausible to suppose that two or
more incompatible secondary theories might cohere ideally well
both internally and with shared primary theory. In that case, if we
assume a coherence theory of truth for secondary theory, we get the
relativistic result that two or more such theories are true.

On which side of the divide between primary and secondary theory do religious beliefs fall? No doubt some theological doctrines ought to be classified as secondary theory. As examples I would cite the medieval doctrine of divine simplicity, according to which there is no composition of any kind in God, and the medieval doctrine of divine eternity, according to which God exists timelessly. Steven Collins has argued that the Buddhist no-self doctrine is to be counted as secondary theory.[3] But are all religious beliefs properly classified as belonging to the domain of secondary theory? In recent philosophy of religion, much has been made of an analogy between microphysical particles such as quarks and spiritual beings such as God.[4] Both, it is said, are unobservable theoretical posits, and both play explanatory roles in virtue of their postulated causal efficacy. If such an explanatory theism were the whole truth, beliefs about God would fall into the category of secondary theory, and thus arguments for semantic relativism there would apply to them and, if sound, show that they have, at best, relative truth.

At the end of his essay, Hollis suggests a way to avoid such conclusions. We might bet, as he seems willing to do, on "the sort of theology that takes the unseen world as a reading of spiritual truths about this world." I am uncomfortable with the reductionistic flavor of this suggestion; it strikes me as too closely allied to the projection theories of religion that originate with Feuerbach's attempt to reduce theology to anthropology. So I am inclined to go in a different direction by pressing the disanalogies between God and quarks. The God of Abraham, Isaac and Jacob, He who covenanted with Israel and often rebuked its infidelity, is very unlike any microphysical particle. The God encountered in Christian mystical experience is being perceived, albeit not sensorily, as William Alston argues in his *Perceiving God*.[5] These considerations lead me to be somewhat suspicious of the sharp distinction between primary and secondary theory in its general application to the religious domain. The distinction was contrived by Horton for the specific purpose of comparing modern science and traditional African religions, and it seems to serve that purpose well enough. It does not follow that it will serve other comparative purposes particularly well. Is there any reason to think it will illuminate more than it obscures when it is used in comparisons of modern science and the major monotheisms? My skepticism on this score makes me tend to believe that it is a considerable oversimplification to say that God is solely and exclusively an object of secondary theory. Thus I am prepared to defend the view that not all beliefs about God belong to secondary theory and that not all of them are threatened by arguments for semantic relativism in the domain of secondary theory.

In concluding, let me lay a couple of my own cards on the table. I am resigned to living with a thoroughgoing epistemic relativism in the realm of religious belief, though I occasionally entertain a wistful hope for convergence in the long run on a rational consensus. However, I am strongly committed to resisting the view that all the beliefs of traditional Christianity achieve no more than relative reference or truth. Accordingly, I am pleased that I find no compelling argument for this view contained in or suggested by the papers of my colleagues.

Notes

1. The example is from an earlier version of Jarvie's essay (Ed.).
2. For more on this topic, see Alasdair MacIntyre, *Whose Justice? Which Rationality?* (Notre Dame: University of Notre Dame Press, 1988) and my review of this book in *Faith and Philosophy* 8 (1991), pp. 109–15.
3. Steven Collins, "What Are Buddhists *Doing* When They Deny the Self?," *Religion and Practical Reason*, ed. Frank Reynolds and David Tracy (Albany: State University of New York Press, forthcoming). See also Steven Collins, *Selfless Persons* (Cambridge: Cambridge University Press, 1982).
4. A good recent discussion is to be found in Michael C. Banner, *The Justification of Science and the Rationality of Religious Belief* (Oxford: Clarendon Press, 1990).
5. William P. Alston, *Perceiving God* (Ithaca and London: Cornell University Press, 1991).

Response
Nicholas Wolterstorff

We all agreed that Philip Quinn's response to our essays, an early version of which he read at our symposium on relativism in religion, made a signal contribution to the discussion. Most of us, in our own responses, have followed Quinn's example and discussed points and themes in the various essays, adding to this our responses to Quinn's criticisms of our own essays. I shall take a different tack and try to advance the discussion by discussing Quinn's discussion.

At the beginning of his response, Quinn distinguishes between "epistemic relativism" and "semantic or metaphysical relativism." The former, he says, "involves the relativization of epistemic statuses," and the latter "involves the relativization of reference or truth or both." But what is meant here by "relativization"?

I suggest that relativism, in all its versions, is a response of a certain type to a situation in which it appears that, or in which claims are made whose conjunction implies that, a given entity at a given time both has and lacks a certain property. Plato struggled over its sometimes apparently being the case that a given thing at a given time both is and is not tall; we in our century are aware of claims that infanticide of certain sorts is a good thing and of claims that infanticide of all sorts is a bad thing. One way of resolving such conflict situations is to come to believe that, counter to one's initial impression, it is really two different entities which are under consideration. Another is to come to believe that it is really two different times which are under consideration. Yet another is to come to believe that it is really two different properties. None of these is a relativist response.

But sometimes none of these three strategies for relief of tension seems at all plausible. That is when the relativist response becomes relevant. The core of the relativist response to such a situation is that what we are really dealing with is not a one-term property but a multi-term relation (or, not a 2-term relation but a 2+n term relation, etc.). Joe is tall relative to Mary but short relative to Herbert. Michael Jr. is son relative to Michael Sr. but father relative to Michael III. Infanticide of defective infants is right relative to the moral code of the ancient Greeks but wrong relative to the moral code of modern day Americans. According to the relativist response, the questions "Is Joe tall or short?", "Is Michael Jr. son or father?", "Is infanticide right or wrong?" are all void for vagueness. Nobody is tall or short *simpliciter* but only *relative* to someone. Nobody is son or father *simpliciter* but only relative to someone. And infanticide is not right or wrong *simpliciter* but only relative to some moral code.

It should be obvious from the foregoing that, with respect to the property of being a relativist, it would be incoherent to be anything other than a relativist. There is no such thing as relativism *simpliciter* but only relative to some property and to some relativizing entity. That relativism is always relative to some property gains clear acknowledgment in Quinn's opening paragraph, where he distinguishes between relativism with respect to such epistemic properties as entitlement to believe (justified in believing) and relativism with respect to truth.

It is my own view that that frustratingly elusive position nowadays called "metaphysical anti-realism" is best interpreted as relativism with respect to truth and existence (and, perhaps, reference). The metaphysical anti-realist claims that the question "Does the snowy egret still exist?" is void for vagueness, as is the question "Is the proposition that the snowy egret still exists true?" Things exist only relative to some conceptual scheme; and propositions are true only relative to some conceptual scheme. Accordingly, only when the scheme is specified do questions of truth and existence have an answer.

Obviously things get rather tangled, if not incoherent, when those who are relativists with respect to normative and evaluative properties are also conceptual-scheme relativists with respect to truth. Then normative and evaluative relativism will not be true or false *simpliciter*, but only relative to some particular conceptual scheme.

Let us now set aside the bulk of properties and relations and confine our attention, for a moment, exclusively to evaluative and normative properties and relations; let us then distinguish relativism concerning the nature of such properties and relations from what I shall call situationalism concerning them. Concerning a given right, obligation, or whatever, it may be one's view that a human being, if she has that right or obligation at all, has it regardless of her contingent situation; alternatively, it may be one's view that she has or lacks it depending on her situation. If the former, one is a non-situationalist with respect to that normative property; if the latter, one is a situationalist with respect to it. Given the history of discussion of these matters, it is important to single out, from all other facets of a person's situation, that facet which consists of the normative and evaluative rules of the person's society.

The normative and evaluative rules of one's society may play a central role both in relativism concerning some normative or evaluative property and situationalism concerning it. Nonetheless, the positions remain distinct. If, for example, a person insists that infanticide is neither right *simpliciter* nor wrong *simpliciter* but only right or wrong relative to some specified set of normative rules, that person is a relativist; if, by contrast, a person insists that infanticide is right in some situations and wrong in others, but then, *in* a given situation, right or wrong *simpliciter*, that person is a situationalist.

Quinn attempts to identify, in the essays of the various symposiasts, epistemic and metaphysical relativism (and opposition thereto) and to appraise whatever arguments may be offered. He describes himself as "resigned to living with a thoroughgoing epistemic relativism in the realm of religious belief," while "strongly committed to resisting metaphysical or semantic relativism concerning such beliefs." But I very much doubt that he is an epistemic relativist concerning such beliefs – not, anyway, on the concept of relativism explained above. He is a situationalist. He thinks that various features of a person's situation enter crucially into whether or not she is entitled to hold some religious belief, but then he thinks that that person in that situation is entitled *simpliciter* to hold that belief or is not entitled *simpliciter* to hold that belief. He doesn't think that that person in that situation is entitled relative to one code and is not entitled relative to another code and that that is the end of the matter. Moving a piece into a certain position on a board is a permissible or an impermissible move only relative to the game being played. Moral and epistemic relativists think of moral and epistemic judgments like that; actions are right or wrong only relative to a particular moral game, believings are right or wrong only relative to a particular doxastic game, and so forth. Quinn, pretty clearly, is not thinking along those lines. For example, speaking of the debate between the Aristotelians and the Kantians, he says that "the adherents of each tradition are within their epistemic rights in having the moral beliefs presently characteristic of that tradition;

those beliefs are rational and fully justified." Those are the words of
a situationalist, as opposed to a relativist, with respect to epistemic
rights, as are these words: "Certain Christians are justified and
quite rational in believing that ultimate reality is personal, i.e., God.
But certain advaitic Hindus are equally justified and rational in
believing that ultimate reality is impersonal, i.e., Brahman. In both
instances, having taken account of both experience and testimony
and having given a fair hearing to objections to their views, these
believers remain within their epistemic rights, so to speak, in
having the religious beliefs they do."

Let me now call attention to yet a third phenomenon in the same
region as those of which we have been speaking, a phenomenon
easily confused with, yet distinct from, the others. Suppose that, for
a certain proposition *P*, we are situationalists with respect to the
property of believing *P* rationally. Then it will be possible for there
to be two people such that one believes *P* and is rational in so doing,
and the other does not believe *P* and is rational in not believing.
Perhaps the latter has not even thought of *P*, or has thought of *P* but
neither believes nor disbelieves, or perhaps he disbelieves. In any
case, there will be one or another form of rational disagreement. But
this phenomenon of rational disagreement, concerning the truth,
say, of infanticide is evil, is different from the position of relativism
with respect to the nature of the property of being evil and is also
different from situationalism with respect to the circumstances
under which some actions of some type have this property. Quite
clearly, however, Quinn, at several points in his discussion, blurs
the difference between rational disagreement, on the one hand, and
relativism and situationalism, on the other. Here is one such
passage, occurring in the course of his discussion of Ian Jarvie's
essay: "I expect the persistence of rational disagreement in religion
as well, particularly among the so-called 'world religions'; they
have, after all, evolved over millennia very complex and sophisticated intellectual defenses or systems of negative apologetics. So I
am willing to bet that epistemic relativism will remain true to some
extent within the realm of religious belief far into the future,
perhaps interminably." Clearly, what Quinn expects to remain
within the realm of religious belief is rational disagreement not epistemic relativism. Of course, the existence of rational disagreement
concerning the truth of some proposition *P* does imply the truth of
situationalism with respect to the rationality of believing *P*.

Quinn is baffled – as I am – by several of the things that Phillips says in his essay. But if metaphysical anti-realism is construed, as I mentioned above I think it should be construed – as concept-scheme relativism concerning truth and existence, then some, though not indeed all, of the baffling things Phillips says can be viewed as expressions of that view and its implications. I especially have in mind Phillips's conclusion, that "religion is relative to the cultural context in which it flourishes, and that God has no existence independent of it," combined with his insistence that believers would not regard the demise of religious practices as entailing the death of God but would instead say that the world had turned its back on God. Quinn interprets Phillips as holding a thesis, or saying things which imply a thesis, concerning conditions for God's existence, namely that God exists only if certain religious practices exist. Phillips, he says, "invites us to suppose that God is no more than a cultural construct, an internal object of human culture." But perhaps Phillips is instead a relativist concerning truth and existence. God exists, indeed, but only relative to certain conceptual schemes, and the proposition that God exists is true relative to, and only relative to, certain conceptual schemes. That relativist claim is quite different from the *situationalist* claim that there are certain situations in which God exists and others in which God does not exist – the situations in question consisting of the existence of theistic conceptual schemes. In those conceptual schemes relative to which God exists, it will not be true that God's existence is contingent on the existence of certain religious practices. Of course, if "God" and its synonyms is not a referring expression, then the issue of God's existence cannot even arise; so my proposal by no means removes all sources of bafflement from Phillips's essay. Phillips appears to me to regard religious language, including theistic language, as lacking in propositional content; the believer, in using language, does not take up one and another illocutionary stance toward some proposition but expresses certain valuings of experience. Such non-cognitivism is yet another position to be distinguished from relativism concerning truth.

Where does all this leave us with respect to the issue of relativism in religion? Well, my own view, upon entering the discussion, was that of a firm anti-relativist with respect to truth and existence and a situationalist, though not a relativist, with respect to entitled (rational, justified) belief. It is my impression that most of my fellow symposiasts were and are of the same view. But the distinctions I have been led to make in reflecting on Quinn's account of our discussions make me no longer entirely sure of that. What would be needed is another go at the same topic.

Responses
I. C. Jarvie

My viewpoint on the philosophy of religion is comparativist. Religious claims are a subset of all claims. (Strictly speaking, the formulation of the previous sentence concedes too much. Religious claims are not a proper subset. All sorts of claims have been labeled religious. The only thing they share is the efforts some people made to draw a category line around them.) If religions are language-games I think of myself as like the compiler of one of those books with titles like *The Complete Book of Board-Game Rules*, well able to grasp the internal logic of the game while still able to discuss whether it is worthwhile playing the game at all. If religion has to do with "the sacred," it is still just another set of claims and liable, like most claims, to be false, however hard that may be to show. Since I view all these and similar proposed lines as demarcations without differences, I tend also to view all religions as potential exhibits in D. Z. Phillips's museum, it being only a matter of time.

Two points raised in discussion provoke me to respond. One concerned the implausibility of my non-justificationist strategy, both in general and as a riposte to relativism. The suggestion was that critical rationalism does not overcome epistemological relativism. To accomplish that task we cannot but advance justifying reasons for our claims and value judgments.

On the face of it this is a forceful objection. From the welter of claims advanced we must needs make a preliminary selection of which to take seriously. No doubt social and personal factors may be involved, even if they should not be. But is it the case that we offer justifying reasons for taking seriously the claims we advance? It was put to me that simply advancing theories and refusing to provide reasons for them was an unconvincing response to relativism.

My answer is that it is unconvincing only because the counter-claim continues to presuppose justificationism and to conclude that absence of justification makes the original claim "unconvincing." Of course, if the following demand is made: "Convince me. And remember, only justifying arguments convince me," then non-justificational critical discussion has been preempted. However, the

ability to convince is not, on a non-justificationist view, an epistemological virtue.

A clear non-justificationist virtue is problem-solving ability. If a
claim makes some headway with a problem, even if that claim has
no persuasive advocates, it deserves our attention. There is a possible price to be paid. It is a price critical rationalism is prepared to
pay: many more unserious and even specious claims have to be tol-
erated than under the justificationist edict. For, as Hollis rightly
notes (p. 132), false and even monstrous views can appear for a
time to be critical and progressive. Feyerabend already noted this
with safe-cracking.[1] Generalizing, we can note that any fideistic
position will permit a good deal of critical leeway and thus may
overlap with or be mistakenly identified with a genuinely critical
position – until criticism is directed at its arbitrary cut-off point or
ultimate assumptions. Thus it is Pickwickian for Hollis to write of
fideistic dogmatisms like Aryan science being "progressive": they
are so only in a strictly circumscribed sense. As Daniel Kevles has
shown,[2] eugenics was scientifically, socially and politically
respectable for a long time. It took a great deal of science to uncover
its error and expose the uncritical way it was held by some who
should then have known better. We must be careful not to use
hindsight on such cases.

My next response is to suggest that our practice is non-
justificationist more often than we realize. Most of the reasons we
put forward when making a claim are not justifications but answers
to anticipated objections; thus they follow the pattern of adjudicating claims by inviting criticism and showing how it can be dealt
with.[3] The claims we take most seriously are those which are criticizable and have been criticized, but not yet successfully. The
present discussion is an example. My argument was that relativism
trades on justificationist presuppositions and constitutes therefore a
criticism of justificationism. This was a reason for proposing non-
justificationism as a solution to the epistemological problem which
gives rise to relativism. Objections have been raised to my claim,
suggesting it does not solve the problems of relativism or of epistemology and that it has internal problems of its own. If my present
"Responses" to the objections have any force, then non-
justificationism deserves a position on the epistemological agenda
for further discussion.

It was also put to me (by Philip Quinn), less as a criticism than as
a conundrum to muse upon, that relativists appear to assume that

something portentous follows from establishing the relativist claim. Grant for a moment a relativist claim, such as "all cognitive and moral claims are epistemologically equal." Does anything interesting follow from this about action or about belief? Does it not leave everybody where they were? That is, even if ultimate justification lies in cultures and all cultures are equal, and even if, therefore, all cognitive and moral claims endorsed by those cultures deserve equal standing, does anything follow for *the relativist's* belief and action?

To philosophers it is glaringly apparent that the practical effect of such relativism is conservative; it "re-endorses," to use Gellner's word, the claims of whoever is giving voice to it. No other claim can be better justified, so my claim is immune to comparativist challenge. However, this also means that I must stick to the claims of my culture. To endorse the claims of another culture would be an arbitrary shift, since they cannot be superior to the claims of my culture and I, as a member of this culture and not of that, can appeal to it as justification and to no other.

To anthropologists this disastrous consequence is not apparent. David Mayberry-Lewis in his "Millennium" television series draws the conclusion that anthropological relativism shows there is something called "tribal wisdom" about which it is urgent we learn.[4] Unlike our learning, theirs is rooted in nature and a balanced relationship with the environment. Their wisdom may contain clues to how we ensure our species' survival. He does not explain how, if all claims are equal, tribes can have superior knowledge, i.e. "wisdom," attributed to them. Another case where anthropological obtuseness displays itself is in the recent exchange between the philosopher Frank Cioffi and the anthropologist Vincent Crapanzano. Reviewing Crapanzano's book, the philosopher exposed some of the recursive absurdities in the anthropologist's relativism:

"The anthropologist has constantly to relativise his own position, to question his basic assumptions about himself and the nature of the world in which he lives." What are these assumptions? And what benefit does Crapanzano anticipate from the development of "other anthropologies coming from other societies with other values"? Does he really want a Samoan account of Moroccan circumcision, a Trobriand account of the Zande chicken oracle, a Zande account of the kula ring, a Moroccan account of growing up in New Guinea? What for? In any case, are these anthropologies not to be enjoined to "relativize" their own positions and to question the "semantico-referentiality" of their own basic assumptions? Would not the extent to which they succeeded preclude there being "other anthropologies with other values"? I don't think Crapanzano has thought this matter through.[5]

Crapanzano wrote an indignant letter summarizing his book, ignoring the criticism, and declaring it a personal attack![6]

Logically speaking, nothing very interesting follows from an assertion of the kind: "all cultures are equal; therefore all cognitive and moral claims endorsed by those cultures are equal too." The example in my paper, then, was a little unfair. The Prime Directive of Star Fleet Command governs the implementation of all operational orders. It bridges the logical gap and converts its relativism into injunctions. My argument was to show that its injunctions did not follow, to show that this was implicitly recognized in the plotting of the teleplays, and to use this to illustrate the misleading plausibility of relativism. That led me to analyze how relativism trades on a weakness of the received epistemology. But it may be sufficient for deromanticizing relativism to show that nothing exciting follows from it. If one believes liberalism follows from it one is mistaken. What follows from it is impotence and appeasement.

Notes

1. P. K. Feyerabend, "Consolations for the Specialist," in I. Lakatos and A. Musgrave, eds, *Criticism and the Growth of Knowledge* (Cambridge: Cambridge University Press, 1970), pp. 197–230, esp. p. 200.
2. Daniel Kevles, *In the Name of Eugenics: Genetics and the Uses of Human Heredity* (New York: Knopf, 1985).
3. The most thorough treatment of why good reasons are neither necessary nor sufficient to advance claims is provided by David Miller in "A Critique of Good Reasons," in Jarvie and Agassi, eds, *Rationality: The Critical View* (Dordrecht: Nijhoff, 1987), pp. 343–58.
4. Most of the claims are made in the first program of the series.
5. Frank Cioffi, "Crisis on Crisis," *Times Literary Supplement*, 24 April 1992, p. 10.
6. Vincent Crapanzano, letter "The Epistemology of Interpretation," *Times Literary Supplement*, 15 May 1992, p. 15.

Perspectives
Martin Hollis

Professor Quinn has traced some themes entwining our diverse essays with consummate skill. At the same time, however, it is evident that we differ in how we construe the character of the relativism which we all reject. Having found the other contributions most instructive on this score, as well as immensely interesting in themselves, I shall start by adding a couple of dimensions to the idea of relativism.

Quinn bids us distinguish firmly between epistemic relativism, which is concerned with warrants for belief, and semantic or metaphysical relativism, which has to do with truth and reference. An epistemic relativist denies that there are absolute or even universal criteria by which to judge the rationality of a belief. There is an undeniable variety of conceptual schemes or "webs of belief." Each comes complete with internal connections which make it rational to accept any particular element, given that one accepts the rest. These internal connections are governed by rules of sound reasoning which apparently vary between schemes. There is no vantage point external to all schemes, from which to judge one conceptual scheme more rational than another. Thus, the epistemic relativist maintains, there are always two ways to defend the rationality of a belief in gods or demons. The more direct is to show that someone who accepts p, q and r is thereby warranted in accepting s by the familiar tests of inductive and deductive logic. (In a scheme where nature is animate and natural events may be the work of unseen agents, it is rational to sacrifice to the god of the sea before making a voyage.) More obliquely, the writ of modern logic may not run everywhere. Perhaps the Trinity holds no mystery for God, because an infinite understanding is unconfined by human laws of thought – a suggestion I shall dispute presently, but tempting for the moment.

A semantic or metaphysical relativist typically refuses to separate questions of what is true or real from questions of what it is rational to believe. Thus Peter Winch declares that "connected with the realisation that intelligibility takes many and varied forms is the realisation that reality has no key" (1958, p. 102). Ontology becomes an implied commitment or consequence of the concepts in use.

Conceptual diversity brings ontological pluralism in its train. Professor Phillips gave the example of chess pieces. There are indeed kings, knights and bishops but only where and while the rules of chess hold sway. The same goes, presumably, for flesh and blood bishops, engendered by episcopal canon. Whether the same holds for gods also is crucial, especially for anyone who insists that there is one true God.

Quinn gives stern warning that one can be an epistemic relativist and yet deny that objects are somehow internal to conceptual schemes and practices. Epistemic relativism does not entail the other kind. It is one question what a statement means and another whether it is true. Hence no thesis about the theory-dependence of facts, even when coupled with pluralism about unrefuted theories, implies that there are as many realities as there are conceptual keys. If relativists want that conclusion, he says, they will need some further premises. I agree in general, although I shall argue later that meaning and truth cannot always be so completely divorced.

Meanwhile it may be useful to note two further dimensions of relativism. Firstly, when truth, meaning or warrants for belief are declared relative, we can ask what they are relative to. Standard answers divide into external and internal. Externally, belief systems are deemed relative to some independent causal system, psychological or social. The usual suggestion is then that the rationale of the belief system lies not in the warrants which the believers themselves cite but in the extraneous system. A Freudian account of religion as sublimation will take this form. Marx gives religion the superstructural function of concealing the economic origins of social relations and values, of legitimating temporal authority by conferring divine benison on it and of consoling the exploited with a prospect of heaven. Durkheim traces the role of religion in sanctifying the social order, enshrining a shared sense of the sacred and policing a vital boundary between the sacred and the profane. Formally such analyses do not imply that gods are a fiction, since a belief may still be true, whatever its origins or functions. But it is worth reflecting that the faithful would stop going to church, if they came to believe that they were only stabilizing their own psyches or sanctifying the social order.

Internally, the idea is that religious belief is relative to itself in a self-sustaining web. Evans-Pritchard put it succinctly when charting the conceptual scheme of the Azande.

In this web of belief every strand depends on every other strand and a Zande cannot get out of its meshes because it is the only world he knows. The web is not an external structure in which he is enclosed. It is the texture of his thought and he cannot think that his thought is wrong. (1937, p. 195)

(Although mesmerically expressed, the observation strikes me as quite false. People often think their thought is wrong.) Similarly, Wittgensteinians readily regard religion as a self-contained practice or "game," where each part makes sense in relation to the rest, but there is no external standpoint from which to query the sense overall. Here too it does not follow formally that there is no exogenous god but, as in Phillips' version, there is no obvious place or need for one. That sounds agnostic. Yet many liberal theologians seem content to internalize the referential claims in sacred texts and I do not wish to be dogmatic about whether God can survive Wittgenstein.

The second dimension emerges when we ask if some beliefs are more relative than others. Moral beliefs are an especially tempting target. The rise of science has tended to cut notions of moral meaning and purpose adrift from those of causal and rational order. Despite eminent attempts at a modern rational ethics, many philosophers have been led to treat moral discourse, as in the previous paragraphs, either as a self-sustained web or functionally. Claims to religious knowledge have, if anything, been a still more tempting target.

For claims to knowledge in general we need to draw a threefold distinction. We are inclined to regard our epistemic beliefs as firmly constrained by facts of experience on the one hand and laws of logic on the other, with beliefs which are more or less probable as negotiable within these limits. *Conceptual relativism* is quick to point out that, since beliefs occupying this intermediate space are underdetermined by logic and experience, they depend on presuppositions or, in some senses of the term, paradigms, which are relative in the ways just discussed. This is a mild contention compared to *perceptual relativism*, which argues from the theory-dependence of facts to the relativity of concepts. As Sapir, for instance, declared, "we see and hear and otherwise experience very largely as we do because the language habits of our community predispose certain choices of interpretation" (1929, p. 209). More boldly still, *logical relativism* contends that even the basic laws of logic are mutable, as did Quine in "Two Dogmas of Empiricism." Winch took this line in *The Idea of a Social Science*, remarking that "the criteria of logic are not a direct gift from God but arise out of and are intelligible in the context of modes of living and of modes of social life" (1958, p. 100).

If truth is the final citadel, these three thrusts will take it unless repulsed. Even conceptual relativism alone is a serious threat, granted the pervasive role of interpretation in belief. If perceptual relativism were to succeed, logic seems too devoid of content to hold the last ditch. If logic is indeed relative, the citadel falls.

All five of us refuse to relativize truth. But we differ about where to dig in. That is partly, no doubt, because we differ about whether to defend any claims to religious knowledge. Professor Jarvie takes the field as a veteran of debates about critical rationalism, who views religion from the flightdeck of the starship *Enterprise* as a form of life which progress has overtaken. He is an epistemic relativist but not a metaphysical one, and he is hard-nosed about what metaphysics permits. Having much admired the imaginative skill with which he steered the *Enterprise*, I hesitate to provoke his lasers. But I remain unconvinced by his thesis that to seek foundations for knowledge is to hand the game to relativism, whereas to trust in a Popperian critical flexibility does not. His case is that any foundationalist stopper to the regress of justification is bound to be dogmatic or arbitrary, whereas "if critical inquiries make progress, then that is the answer to relativism." Since he is an epistemic relativist, however, "progress" will presumably be a matter of a discourse which develops coherently through discussion. By this test many pernicious theories rise above relativism, for example Aryanism, which under the Third Reich developed an organized body of reasoned propositions between its fanatical or cynical origins and its arrival at the Final Solution. On the other hand, it is not obvious to me that foundationalist statements are all dogmatic or arbitrary. Kantian attempts at transcendental arguments are not yet exhausted.

I treasure the image of Professor Phillips hurrying past the gods of the Upper Nile and pausing to wonder whether the Christian God will one day join them in a dusty corner of the museum. He concludes reassuringly that no gods are ever to be found in museums because gods exist only in the intercourse of their worshippers. They are not objects to be named but belong to a living grammar of religious language. This strongly suggests that they die when their erstwhile worshippers die out or lose interest in them and turn to talk of other things. If so, the position is clearly relativist. But Phillips takes a final stand on the difference between epistemic and metaphysical relativist, presumably so that a true god might survive cultural eclipse. But, I am bound to say, this last ditch is precarious after his likening of the gods of Egypt to the pieces in chess. That does indeed explain why the pieces of defunct games which find their way into museums are but husks of practices and hence not truly pieces in a game. Yet one notes that chess, like senat (an ancient Egyptian game whose rules are now obscure), is wholly a human construct. The analogy gives metaphysical relativism all it wants, and when Phillips claims to exhibit "the grammar of our use of God," Sir Jacob Astley would certainly dispute it. For Sir Jacob, "God" was clearly a name – a different "grammar" which Phillips cannot condemn as confused without falling out with the faithful.

This is not to say that Phillips is wrong about the "grammar" of religion. I contend only that if he is right, then relativism prevails. But I recognize a risk of begging a hard question about the relation of meaning to reference, a question which also arises in the other essays. Admittedly Professor Wolterstorff and Professor Quinn speak as commentators and not in their own voices. They have made it clear how they mean to halt relativism, however, especially in the discussion afterwards.

Wolterstorff's fascinating account of Hans Frei ends with some remarks of his own, including a doubt whether the interpretation of utterances can proceed without regard to their truth. For instance, truth is involved in deciding whether to take an utterance literally or metaphorically. I agree. The general position has to be that texts make good sense, for the most part, when construed aright and that lapses from good sense can be confidently identified against a background of good sense which makes them plausible. At any rate this is the assumption on which Wolterstorff proceeds. Yet must we not also agree with Winch that intelligibility takes many and varied forms? Although the short answer is yes, since the diversity of beliefs is undeniable, the deep answer is, I believe, no. The effect of complete open-mindedness would be impenetrable hermeneutic circles. If it were wholly an empirical question what someone not only meant and believed true but also took as the criterion of good sense and good reason, then no interpretation would be more defensible than any other. This is the nub of the "bridgehead" argument for universally presupposed criteria by which to ensure the meeting of minds.

That gives no clue to what sort of presuppositions we need for understanding religion. Professor Quinn, to judge from his endorsement of John Hick, favors a "noumenal Real," resistant to both conceptual and moral relativism. In Kantian vein, he opines that all religions offer a transforming path to salvation, this being less a fact of observation than, I fancy, a putatively synthetic *a priori* truth. I applaud the strategy. But his "noumenal Real" seems too sketchy by far. Thus, since some religions and theologies posit a personal god and others do not, the noumenal real is noncommittal about that. Since religions differ about whether god is one or many, the noumenal real is silent here too. One quickly begins to suspect that the idea is too abstract to serve as an answer to the Kantian question "What makes religion possible?" But perhaps Quinn can find ways to fill in his sketch. I hope so.

Taking a cue from my reference to Robin Horton's distinction between primary and secondary theory, he suggested in the discussion that, although religions clearly include divergent secondary theories, they share a primary core. That sounds promising. For instance, medieval Christianity had ideas about God and time which are secondary in Horton's sense but this does not stop us arguing that every religion shares an ontology which assigns gods and quarks to different orders of being. What, then, divides primary from secondary? Part of the answer, I suggest, is that primary theories fuse epistemology and metaphysics. That is why I demurred earlier about whether meaning and truth can always be kept apart. Lurking behind the claim that religions are to be understood by recognizing a common primary theory is an ontological argument to the effect that to understand the religious angle of vision is to share its essential presuppositions.

I conclude that, although false beliefs can be rational, not all rational beliefs can be false. But this is meant to imply only the vaguest of theisms. So I feel free to hurry Phillips through all the religious galleries in the museum, to put it to Jarvie that the liberal First Directive is not relativist at all, and to join the liberal humanists in the tea room.

References

Evans-Pritchard, E. E., *Witchcraft, Oracles and Magic among the Azande* (Oxford: Clarendon Press, 1937).
Sapir, E., "The status of linguistics as a science," *Language*, 5 (1929).
Winch, P., *The Idea of a Social Science* (London: Routledge & Kegan Paul, 1958).

Philosophers' Clothes
D. Z. Phillips

A man once made a terrible mistake: he turned up at a fancy-dress party in his ordinary clothes. But he needn't have worried. The other guests welcomed him warmly. "How ingenious! You've come as a man in ordinary clothes."

In relation to my fellow-symposiasts at the conference, I felt like the man in the ordinary clothes. They insisted that, despite my claims to the contrary, I must be in some form of metaphysical dress: epistemic relativist, semantic relativist, metaphysical relativist, fideistic relativist, phenomenal realist, noumenal realist, naturalist, critical rationalist. No one could deny the variety in the wardrobe. The appearances were impressive in a certain way, so perhaps it was not surprising that it was thought that I *must* have been dressed for the occasion.

Now my aim was not to put on fancy dress but to get the ordinary recognized. But this is easier said than done. Fancy dress keeps getting in the way. Kierkegaard tells a story about dress which illustrates the point. One day he wanted to get his suit pressed. He took it to a shop which had a sign in the window: "Suits Pressed Here." But he came out of the shop disappointed: only the sign was for sale. The story is suggestive in two ways.

First, in saying that the sign was for sale, the story suggests that there is a market for purchasing signs. Although the sign would normally indicate that work could be expected, the purchaser becomes more interested in the sign. This is because such signs, divorced from practice, become endowed with a commendatory force, while their opposites inherit a denigratory force. This baptism of signs in philosophy hinders the work of conceptual clarification. Here is a list of signs that have accrued these associations in contemporary philosophy of religion.

Commendatory signs: realist, factual, cognitive, objective, referential, rational. Denigratory signs: non-realist, non-factual, expressive, relative, non-referential, fideistic. A philosopher is held to be giving a good account of what is meant by God's reality if the commendatory signs can be applied to it. Thus, it is good to say that "There is a God" is a factual, referential assertion, with cognitive and propositional content, which has, as its object, a real, objective, non-relative substance or entity. What a happy combination of signs that is! But it is magically happy. It creates a feeling of intellectual ease which is unearned. This sense of ease is shared by atheistic opponents impressed by the same signs. They concur that, in order to be true, religious belief needs to be baptized by such signs. Of course, they differ from their religious counterparts in denying that any such baptism can ever be legitimate.

What happens if denigratory signs are ascribed to an account of God's reality? What if it is said that "There is a God" is not a referential, factual assertion and that its relative meaning shows its expressive content does not have a substance or entity as its object? Unsurprisingly, this combination of signs is called "reductionist" and unhappy. But, once again, it is magically happy. The unhappy combination is said to be compatible with atheism but incompatible with theism. A view called Wittgensteinian fideism is said, incredibly, to actually offer the unhappy combination of signs as an analysis of religious belief. But, as I shall try to show, this ascription of signs, commendatory or denigratory, is magical; it is unmediated via any conceptual elucidation or clarification.

To substantiate this conclusion we need to turn to the second suggestive aspect of Kierkegaard's story. The sign in the window, "Suits Pressed Here," although for sale, and no matter how prestigious its possession becomes, *actually does not do the work it promises to do.* In that sense it is an idle sign, or a sign of idleness. No suits get pressed. The same is true in contemporary philosophy of religion. The signs do not work, so nothing is clarified. When conceptual clarification occurs, the signs have only a secondary importance.

Let us illustrate my claims with respect to whether talk of God's reality is talk of a matter of fact. In order to bring out important conceptual differences between our talk of the reality of physical objects and our talk of God's reality, a philosopher may say that to talk of God's reality is not to talk of a matter of fact. For those impressed by commendatory signs, this is upsetting since non-factual is a denigratory sign. "Non-factual" is taken to be the equivalent of "unreal." I said in my essay: "The kind of talk which is influencing us is that in which we refer to the same person, the same church, the same planet, etc. But when we look at how we would establish identities in these contexts, we see that nothing of this kind enters into considerations as to whether two people worship *the same God*" (p. 5). The philosopher has in mind what is involved in our talk of empirical facts when we speak of "finding out the facts," "checking the facts," "indicating the fact," and so on. So when he says that God's reality is not "factual," he is not denying reality to the divine. On the contrary, he is interested in elucidating the grammar of "divine reality," in what the distinction between the real and the unreal comes to in this context. He is showing that God's reality is a spiritual reality.

But now suppose some other philosopher feels that dropping the sign is fatal, that it is essential to call God's reality "factual." What then? Should we begin a war over signs, insisting that the sign be dropped? Not at all. But do not forget that the sign, as such, is *lifeless*; it achieves nothing. It comes to life in *practice*, in what is done with it. In "A Prayer for Understanding" Hollis says that believers in a divine scheme express "a firm conviction that there are facts of the matter" (p. 16) and that the church will sink "unless some of its adherents find some of its doctrine simply and evidently true" (p. 16). But what does it mean to speak of "the facts of the matter" in this context, or to speak of something as "simply and evidently true"? Nothing is clarified if we offer abstract tautologies in reply, as Wolterstorff does when he says "if I am making claims about some person Jesus, then I am referring to him and predicating something of him; and the proposition I express is true if and only if *he* exists and has the property I predicated of him" ("Will Narrativity Work as Linchpin?", pp. 103f). It is not the above tautology which throws light on practice but the details of practice which throw light on what saying it amounts to in the particular case. Thus we shall have to discuss whether this is the same no matter whether Jesus is called the son of Mary or whether he is called the Son of God, whether we say he worked at Joseph's right hand in the carpenter's shop, or whether we say that he sits at the right hand of God the Father.

In his "Comments" Quinn says:

As it is typically used in theistic discourse, the term 'God' may indeed not be a proper name in some of the technical senses now current in analytic philosophy of language.... All these are very interesting technical questions. But however they may be answered, one thing seems abundantly clear. In the usage of the vast majority of traditional theists, the term 'God' functions as a

referring expression of some sort, and the object to which theists
mean to refer by using it transcends all human cultures. Thus, far
from being relatively innocent descriptive observations about the
grammar of the term 'God,' the remarks Phillips makes on this
topic are, and ought to be recognized as, deeply radical proposals
for revision in traditional theistic linguistic practices. (Pp. 113f)

But when Quinn says that "God" is a referring expression of
some sort, of *what* sort? We might say that "pain" functions as a
referring expression. But not every object of reference is an object.
Wittgenstein says that "pain" is not "something," yet adds, "but
not a 'nothing' either." Does it help to counter this by saying that
"pain" is sort of "something"? What is important is not to do battle
over signs but to point out grammatical differences in our practices.
Wittgenstein says: "Of course, what confuses us is the uniform
appearance of words when we hear them spoken or meet them in
script and print. For their *application* is not presented to us so
clearly. Especially when we are doing philosophy!" (*Philosophical
Investigations* I, par.11). In the battle of the signs we need to heed
the following warning: "When we say: 'Every word in language
signifies something' we have so far said *nothing whatsoever*; unless
we have explained exactly *what* distinctions we wish to make"
(ibid., par.13).

In order to make important distinctions between our talk about
physical objects and our talk about God, it has been said that the
latter is not a factual matter. Kierkegaard said that God does not
exist, he is eternal. Simone Weil said that in loving God we love
something that does not exist. God is more important than anything which could be said to exist. But if what Kierkegaard and
Simone Weil say does not help; if it proves more of a hindrance
than a help, then by all means say that "God" functions as a referring expression, that "God" refers to a sort of object, that God's
reality is a matter of fact, and so on. *But please remember that, as yet,
no conceptual or grammatical clarification has taken place.* We have all
the work still to do since we shall now have to show, in this religious context, what speaking of "reference," "object," "existence,"
and so on amounts to, how it differs, in obvious ways, from other
uses of these terms. It is in the light of these differences that one has
to decide whether using such signs is more of a hindrance than a
help. Our task is not to baptize practices with signs, since it is
within our practices that the signs have their life. If we try to give

signs a meaning independent of our practices we shall be guilty of what Wittgenstein called "subliming the logic of our language."[1]

There are instances of subliming the logic of our language, it seems to me, in the essays of my fellow symposiasts. For example, Quinn wants to distinguish between epistemic relativism, on the one hand, and semantic or metaphysical realism, on the other. By the former, he means pessimism about reaching a consensus with respect to our rational and justified beliefs. I may be justified in telling someone that there is a chair next door because I have just seen it there, or I may have put it there a few minutes ago. What I say is perfectly rational. Yet, of course, this is quite compatible with my belief being false. In the short time which has elapsed since I saw the chair or placed it in the room, someone, unknown to me, may have taken the chair away. But why should this lead us to speak of a distinction between epistemic relativism and metaphysical or semantic realism, meaning by the latter a use of "real" or "true" which is independent of any epistemic context whatsoever? What has been shown to be false in my example is a *specific* belief about the chair. It is shown to be false in terms of our familiar language about physical objects. That language is not itself a hypothesis about anything. The harmless nature of *one* form of relativism (though even here the term does more harm than good) is simply the obvious truth that in order to understand what the distinction between true and false beliefs means, we must look to the language within which the beliefs are expressed and have their sense. In the case of our language about physical objects, as elsewhere, it involves *activity*, in this case, looking, touching, fetching, sitting on, cutting up, smelling, etc., etc. To seek a use of "true" and "real" independent of all such contexts is an example of subliming the logic of our language. To embrace this conclusion, it is said, is to be a semantic, metaphysical or conceptual relativist. So instead of the argument being pursued, one's analysis gets a bad name by a baptism of denigratory signs.

The context in which Quinn pursues his distinction between epistemic relativism and metaphysical realism is one which arises from John Hick's treatment of religious pluralism. "According to Hick," Quinn tells us, "what the great religions have in common is that each offers a path to salvation which involves a transformation of human existence from self-centeredness to reality-centeredness. As far as we can tell, all of these traditions are of roughly equal effectiveness in producing this transformation" ("Religious Pluralism and Religious Relativism," p. 36). Let me say, in passing, that this conclusion is premature. For example, detailed attention is needed to see how similar or different are conceptions of "losing the self" in different religions. If there are important differences, the notions of salvation will be correspondingly different. Hence, the great religions could not be seen as different paths to the *same* salvation, but as offering different conceptions of salvation. Such a variety is found, it seems to me, not only between religions, but within religions which carry the same name. But let this objection pass. The rough equivalence assumed, we are told: "this suggests the hypothesis that a single ultimate reality 'is being differently conceived and therefore differently experienced and therefore differently responded to from within our different religio-cultural ways of being human'" (ibid., p. 36). Notice the shift from specific beliefs, as in my example of the chair, to epistemic contexts as such, where these are now treated as hypotheses about an ultimate reality. But no context has been given in which this notion of "ultimate reality" can be given sense. Quinn endeavors to give it a context, one which avoids, he thinks, any semantic, metaphysical or conceptual relativism:

> Sentences that are alleged to express schema-relative truths about the noumenal Real are best seen as abbreviations for sentences that express non-relative truths about relations between the noumenal Real and various conceptual schemes. In other words, talk about schema-relative truths about the noumenal Real is acceptable only because it can be analyzed away in terms of talk about non-relative truths about relations between the noumenal Real and the schemas in which it manifests itself. (Ibid., p. 45)

My contention is going to be that language has taken wing, as Plato says, in these notions of the noumenal Real and its alleged activity of manifesting itself in our conceptual schemes. The notion of "the sober metaphysical truth" is a conceptual chimera and can be given no application. Hollis recognizes that this whole issue involves "a hard question about the relation of meaning to reference" ("Perspectives," p. 133).

The philosophical context for the exploration of this question in Hick's work is borrowed from Kant. It is expounded by Quinn as follows:

Speaking in Kantian terms, we may describe this ultimate reality as the Real *an sich* or the noumenal Real. It does not possess the features typically attributed to ultimate reality by the great religious traditions.... This does not mean that there is nothing we can say about the Real *an sich;* it falls under certain purely formal concepts such as the concept of being beyond the scope of other than purely formal concepts.... Hence the noumenal Real must be presumed not to fall under the other than purely formal concepts that shape the thought and experience of the great religious traditions. ("Religious Pluralism and Religious Relativism", pp. 36–7)

Looking at the world religions, we can say

there are therefore several phenomenal Reals, all of which are appearances or manifestations of the same noumenal Real.... On a naturalistic interpretation of religion, according to which there is no noumenal Real, the various phenomenal Reals of the religious traditions would be illusory because they would reduce to purely human projections." (Ibid.)

It seems, then, that the noumenal Real is the subject of all that can be predicated truly. Hick insists that the subject is purely formal. How, then, are we to refer to it? It seems that we have to do so by some such phrase as "Reality in itself" or the ultimate "This." This latter suggestion is not meant to be flippant, since the demonstrative pronoun plays a beguiling role in sending our words into orbit beyond the reach of sense. Think of the way it enters into our teaching of concepts: "This is a tree," "This is called red," "This is what we mean by 'two'," and so on. But, as Wittgenstein points out, the demonstrative pronoun "this" does not, of itself, establish sense or reference: "an ostensive definition can be variously interpreted in *every* case" (*Investigations* I, par.28). Someone teaching "two" by saying "This is two nuts" may be taken as referring to the nuts. Wittgenstein asks whether such difficulties can be overcome by saying "This *number* is two," "This *color* is called red," "This *length* is called a meter," and so on. But, then, this takes for granted that we know how to use the words "number," "color" and "length": "so one might say: the ostensive definition explains the use – the meaning – of the word when the overall role of the word in the language is clear. Thus, if I know that someone means to explain a colour-word to me, the ostensive definition 'That is called sepia,' will help me to understand the word" (ibid.). So the use of "this" does not transcend our practices, our use of it. The "this" Hick and Quinn want to refer to is the noumenal Real, ultimate reality. Wittgenstein says: "yet, strange to say, the word 'this' has been called the only *genuine* name; so that anything else we call a name was only one in an inexact, approximate sense" (*Investigations* I, par.38). Think of how Hick and Quinn speak of the phenomenal Reals as appearances or manifestations of the noumenal Real. The noumenal real, like the ultimate "this," can never be shown to have a nature. Hollis complains that the "'noumenal Real' seems too sketchy by far" ("Perspectives", p. 134) and hopes that Quinn will be able to fill out the sketch. But the sketchiness is not accidental; it cannot be filled out because it is the product of conceptual confusion. Consider the subject–predicate proposition "The table is brown." We can construct a second proposition in which the subject of the first sentence appears as a predicate: "This physical object is a table." But what of the proposition "This is a physical object"? It would be a mistake to think that "this" refers to a name alongside "brown," "table" and "physical object." You can say "This is an N," where N will be a name, but there are no definitions of the form "This is called 'this'." By thinking otherwise, one can be led to think that all possible descriptions will ultimately be about "this," the only ultimate name. All possible names will seem approximations. They never exhaust the nature of "this", which is beyond them all. At this point, Wittgenstein says that language is idling; it has gone on holiday. The attempted use of "this" does not refer to anything at all. By making it independent of all practice, it ceases to be a genuine name.

The same can be said of Hick's noumenal Real. Placed by him beyond all divine names, it, too, is not a name at all. There is something we can call number. There is something we call color. There is something we call banking. There is something we call honesty. There is something we call God. It would be utterly confused to conclude from this that there must be "something," which manifests itself in all these ways. It is not "something" that endows these various practices with sense but our practices which give a point to saying, on occasion, "There is something we call...." So the proposition "The noumenal Real manifests itself as ..." is an *entirely* unmediated form of words; it is meaningless. For Quinn, it seems, religions are illusory if there is no noumenal Real. He thinks that the rejection of this metaphysical notion reduces all religions to the status of human projections. But, as Wittgenstein says, all we have rejected is a grammatical fiction, a house of cards.

I tend to think that, as a matter of fact, Hick was not led into confusions concerning the noumenal Real via these problems in philosophical logic. I think his prior theological commitments led him to make a certain use of Kantian metaphysics. He wants world religions to respect each other, and his metaphysical scheme subserves that end. But, as we have seen, the metaphysical words are winged words. They have no context of application and, therefore, no sense. Hick's hopes for mutual respect, tolerance and learning are found a home, I believe, in the belief in a high God, or a God above all gods, found in some religions. But this is already a religious notion. It is not at all clear how the attitudes this notion generates could ever emanate from the purely formal idea of the noumenal Real. Whether two people are worshipping the same God is itself a religious question. If we believe in a God above all gods, this is one way of expressing the spiritual conviction that no one has a monopoly of the truth. We may find the same spirit in other religions, or, finding something different there, one may find one's own sense of the spiritual being extended. These are not second-best contexts we have to settle for but the living contexts in which these issues have their sense. Quinn and Hick turn religious growth and development into a metaphysical mystery. Quinn, therefore, has to conclude: "I am resigned to living with a thoroughgoing epistemic relativism in the realm of religious belief, though I occasionally entertain a wistful hope for convergence in the long run on a rational consensus. However, I am strongly committed to resisting the view that all the beliefs of traditional Christianity achieve no more than relative reference or truth" ("Comments," p. 118). Perhaps here, too, a prior religious commitment to tolerance and humility in the search for spiritual truth has led to a metaphysical dead-end. The phrase "There are ... several phenomenal Reals, all of which are appearances or manifestations of the same noumenal Real" ("Religious Pluralism and Religious Relativism," p. 37) seems a distant echo of "God, who at sundry times and in diverse manners spoke in times past unto the fathers by the prophets, Hath, in these last days spoken unto us. . . . " The religious conviction has an application; the metaphysical conviction has not. The world religions attempt to bring near what might appear to be far off. The effect of Hick's Kantian schema and of Quinn's treatment of the distinction between epistemic relativism and metaphysical realism is to make what is religiously near a distant and confused metaphysical thesis.

At this stage, I fear, a certain general thesis will be attributed to me, one which says that I settle for "schema-relative truth" to the neglect of "the sober metaphysical truth." Hollis and Jarvie may well accuse me of saying that while mistakes can be made within practices, we cannot speak of practices themselves as confused or mistaken. Examples will be produced to show how there can be, and have been, pervasive practices which were, nevertheless, confused. But who would dispute this? Only fictional fideists who are a product of the critics' imagination.[2] What is missed in these examples is that practices are shown to be confused in terms of some other practice, in terms of what we do. In other words, confusion does not occur *in vacuo*. The appropriate epistemic context shows us the *kind* of confusion it is. Without such contexts our talk of confusion would have no sense. If someone thinks that all such contexts could be called confused, he has the task of telling us what he means. What "confusion" comes to varies with the epistemic context in question. For example, in religion it would be a confusion to say that one could hide from God, as Adam attempted to do among the trees of the Garden of Eden. It would be a further confusion if someone attempted to explain this impossibility in terms of God's super-eyesight! This distorts the grammar of "God sees all things."

The epistemic contexts are not something we must learn to live with, given the unavailability of the noumenal Real, but, rather, they are the contexts in which distinctions between the real and the unreal have their sense. At various points in "A Prayer for Understanding" Hollis makes remarks like the following: "But no one in the front line will grant that God is a *purely internal object of belief*. Astley's prayer is couched in a typically *objective mode* and has a *firmly external address*" (p. 20, my italics). Again, as in Quinn's case, "purely internal" is made to sound like a restriction, whereas I am simply referring to the varied contexts in which words have their application. To seek a use for "internal," "objective," and "external" which transcends these contexts is to sublime the logic of our language.

Think of ways within religion in which distinctions between the objective and the subjective are drawn. Think of the claims by over-eager converts relating to spectacular religious experiences. Wiser spiritual judgments may well conclude that their claims say more about themselves than about God. These conclusions are themselves religious and spiritual judgments. What else could they be? Hollis may say I am ignoring hard cases, for example the "objective" and "external" language of Sir Jacob Astley's prayer. As we shall see, I am not convinced by Hollis's reading of it, but let us suppose he is right. In that case, you may have a conception of God which can be criticized in various ways. For example, Simone Weil says: "what do you tell a child if you want to explain to him that he should never tell lies? If the family is a religious one, one will explain to the child that God knows everything. This answer to the child's question makes a policeman of God. Obedience which is understood in this way is not a virtue."[3] Hollis has Astley make a C.O. of God and the consequences are similar. They will be at one with those who could tell bereaved mothers after the Second World War that had they prayed harder their sons would have come home. Astley's prayer, "Lord, Thou knowest that I must be very busie this day. If I forget Thee, do not Thou forget me," may mean something very different. There is a play on two uses of the word "forget." In the busyness of battle Sir John may well not be thinking about God, if by that is meant having conscious thoughts about him. But he does not want God to forget him, to be distanced from him in the battle. What distances us from God is sin. Even in battle Sir John's prayer is that, in his conduct, he will not forget that he and his enemies are children of God. If the prayer does mean that, it is a striking one, addressed to a Father, not a C.O., in heaven. It would be far removed from the battle-cry of the Covenanters, "For Jesus, and no quarter!"

It is hard to know where Hollis stands overall on these matters, for at the end of his essay he says that his own conjecture is that "the truth lies in a rapprochement between humanism and the sort of theology which takes the unseen world as a reading of spiritual truths about this world" (p. 33). This may or may not be a promising start, and Quinn is suspicious of its reductionist flavor. In any case, on Hollis's reading of him, it would not please Sir John. But, then, why should it? Religion is a mixed bag involving different levels of spirituality, along with plenty of examples of worldly power deified.

In my defense of epistemic contexts as the contexts in which concepts have their life and sense, I hope I have said enough to convince Jarvie, as my essay obviously failed to do, that such a defense will not lead to the consequences he ascribes to relativism. In "The Justificationist Roots of Relativism" he says: "My theme in this paper is that these relativist values are false to practice and false to our values. The reason why is simple: relativism is a poor excuse for refusing to take responsible decisions."[4] He concludes his

"Responses" by saying of relativism: "What follows from it is impotence and appeasement" (p. 128). Why does Jarvie come to this conclusion? Is it true that recognizing conceptual variety in morals leads to shirking decisions, impotence and appeasement? Part of the answer may be his assumption that such recognition involves giving equal value to all practices and cultures. No doubt some relativists have talked in this way, but in doing so have they not contradicted themselves? Claiming that there is no common measure by which all practices and cultures can be assessed, they promptly belie the claim by saying that they have equal value, a view which is itself a measurement of them. Given a variety of moral perspectives, reactions to them will differ. I see no reason for thinking that the mere existence of other perspectives should make me doubt my own. If I come to think I am mistaken, that mistake will be elucidated in other moral terms, the different ones I have appropriated. I do not see that Hollis's notion of primary theory would do much to address the fundamental differences which arise. Our moral responsibility will show itself in our facing or evading challenges and difficulties. But differences may remain. They are not the shadows of the rational consensus Quinn some- times finds himself longing for. The moral differences are what they are, and they divide us. How people view these differences and divisions also varies enormously. The differences are there like our lives, and moral responsibility gets its sense, partly, in how we face them.

Jarvie, quite rightly, wants to reject all-embracing endorsements of practices, whether they belong to other cultures or our own. He wants to subject them to piecemeal criticism. Unfortunately, his own conception of such criticism is fed by a one-sided diet of exam- ples. For him, religion does not solve practical problems, and that is that. Jarvie does not flap his arms, he gets on aeroplanes like the rest of us. But, then, Wittgenstein reminds us that primitive peoples did not pray for sun at night; they lit lamps like everyone else. Neither do they dance for rain outside the rainy season. They dance when the rains are due. The dances celebrate the coming of the rain. Before we start attributing more signs to this account, calling it "emotive," "attitudinal," "expressive," and so on, please note that the dance, the celebration, made a difference to what the coming of rain meant for these people. Would it not be philistinism if someone were to say "Dance or no dance, you still get wet"? One might as well say that our conception of the dead remains essentially the same whether we conduct burial services or whether we put them out with the garbage. After all, they're dead aren't they? Jarvie's optimism regarding an eventual consensus on moral matters is, as Quinn says, misplaced. He says that Jarvie's "example of wanton cruelty being wrong is unfortunate because it involves an analytic truth" ("Comments," p. 112). Difficulties and differences emerge when we consider particular cases. Consider a tribe whose warrior values are highly esteemed. To be captured in battle is a form of dishonor. This dishonor is overcome via rituals of respect by the captors. Let us say that the captured warrior is tied to a tree and prodded with hot sticks. He bears the pain without flinching. This act of respect, it seems to me, cannot be equated with torture. Neither the captors nor the captives think in these terms. The ritual is one in which the distinction between victor and vanquished is transcended in the act of respect. The captor does not gloat, and the captive is not humiliated. Yet, having understood the meaning relative to the ritual, a number of reactions is still open to an observer. Someone may admire warrior values and regret their decline or demise in his own society. But someone else, despite understanding the ritual, may be against it because of what is considered its unnecessary infliction of pain. Respect, it might be said, could and should take another form. Again, another observer, noting the difference between cruelty and the act of respect, may not feel the need to make any judgment of the ritual. Again, the possibility of different moral reactions shows that the recognition of different moral perspectives need not lead to an avoidance of moral responsibility, impotence of judgment or any form of appeasement.

Given these different moral reactions to rituals which manifest distinctive concepts, I find no grounds for Jarvie's general thesis that it is only a matter of time before science and the social sciences reduce all religions to curiosities in our museums. Critical inquiry will no doubt reveal confused rituals, but Jarvie's generalization cannot be defended. For Quinn, as we have seen, the defense against naturalistic accounts of religions which attempt to reduce them to human projections depends on the existence of the noumenal Real. Having attacked that metaphysical notion, the defense against naturalistic reductions of religion clearly must be sought elsewhere. It can be found in the fact that the history of anthropological, sociological and psychoanalytic attempts to explain away religion wholesale is singularly unimpressive. In these attempts the

disciplines often infringe the presuppositions of their own method-
ologies. This is notoriously the case with Freud.[5] If Jarvie wants to
argue for the possibility of a *general* reductionist critique of religion,
he will have to provide far more examples than he, in fact, provides. But I do not see how countless examples of religious practices can be explained away.

Given what I have said about the diversity of moral and religious
perspectives and the equally diverse moral and religious reactions
to them, it should be clear why philosophy cannot be the source or
arbiter of truth in these matters. In "A Prayer for Understanding"
Hollis seems to recognize this when he says: "Questions of truth
soon become nuanced, as one comes to wonder first whether
'knowledge' has a logic relevant to all religious belief and practice,
then whether 'truth' is univocal between rationalists and mystics
and then how exactly different religions are in competition, especially given ecumenical hopes that all are in search of the same
god" (p. 18). Yet he goes on to say immediately: "But the day of
judgment awaits and will settle these matters, unless, of course,
atheists were right all along." Putting aside the misleading implication that to confront God is to confront some kind of object, how is
this eschatological verification supposed to bear on the moral
matters Hollis has in mind? In my essay I argued that such a con-
frontation could not guarantee a transition from self-centered pru-
dence to moral concern, or a transition from one moral perspective
to another. A further argument is needed, one by which an "object"
can be guaranteed to generate an appropriate response to itself. No
such argument can be provided. Eschatological verification of the
kind envisaged cannot be used to arbitrate between moral and religious practices.

If questions of sense cannot transcend our practices, Quinn
thinks it follows that God could not be said to survive the demise of
the linguistic practice in which talk of God has its sense. Quinn
says: "But if the believer is mistaken in thinking that the term 'God'
refers to something that transcends all human cultures, the believer
is also mistaken in thinking or saying that God would survive the
demise of certain cultural practices" ("Comments," p. 114). This
worry is based on a confusion. What I have argued is that unless
we appreciate the way the word "God" is used in religious practice,
we cannot appreciate *the sense* in which we cannot say that God has
died, even if there were no believers. This is not an exceptional
thesis devised for religion. Unless we appreciate the sense in which

we speak of physical objects, we will not appreciate, either, the sense in which mountains existed before there were human beings. Quinn tries to transcend these contexts in which words have their life and sense. He says that if Christianity were to cease to exist, "the upshot would be the sad loss of many true beliefs about ultimate reality, beliefs that are non-relativistically true and not just true for Christians or in Christendom" ("Comments," p. 115). We have already seen the vacuity of this notion of "ultimate reality." Further, if by "non-relativistically true" Quinn means a conception of truth which does not have its sense in some practice or other, it will turn out to be just as vacuous.[6] Quinn says that God will see to it that Christianity will not cease to exist. This notion of "seeing to it" is also vacuous, since it lacks any context of application. It is a magical or superstitious use of "seeing to it."[7] In my essay I did offer a positive account of what would be the case, from a religious point of view, if Christianity were to cease to exist: it would be a case of the world turning its back on God. If we believe this, it would not be considered to be a truth for Christians only, or a truth operative only within Christendom.

Semantic realism is the view that what we mean by "true" is always the same, whether we are talking of a true account of how many chairs there are in a room, or talking of true love. The view is confused. Unless we recognize different grammars of "true," we will not be able to understand central Christian beliefs. I agree with Wolterstorff that there is an essential difference between historical fictions and history. It is extremely important to Christians whether Jesus actually existed. An actual crucifixion is obviously different from a historical fiction concerning a crucifixion. It is the same person who is crucified, who is then raised on high, exalted. Unless Jesus departed he could not be received again in the Holy Spirit. As Rush Rhees has pointed out, this was part of the rejection of the Jewish conception of the Messiah, one who would come to found a historical kingdom.[8] But, then, in speaking of the coming of the Holy Spirit, we have to distinguish between the reality of the dead and the reality of the living. If Jesus had not existed, he could not have been crucified. But we cannot say, without grammatical variation, that unless he continued to exist, Jesus could not come again in the Holy Spirit. To think he could would be an attempt at transcendentalizing the Jewish conception of the Messiah. That Jesus existed is a historical truth, answerable to historical criteria of verification. That the Holy Spirit was

received is not such a truth, and it would make no sense to speak
of it being assessed by historical criteria.

Whether such conceptual clarification works or not in this particular case, such clarification was certainly the aim of the
conference, as far as I was concerned, with respect to the various
issues concerning religion and relativism. In "A Prayer for
Understanding" there are times when Hollis entertains far more
ambitious expectations: "We come together not for a potlatch but to
seek the truth about claims to religious knowledge.... Those who
depart no wiser because they sought no wisdom may have enjoyed
a potlatch generously provided by our hosts but will have been
playing a different game, that of taking a holiday on expenses. I
stress that the conference is a truth-seeking game.... Its question is,
in effect, whether anything worth saying about 'religious knowledge' can be said without inquiry into the implications of removing
the quotation marks. If it can, I submit, the conference will have
been a sham"(p. 30). The first half of these remarks suggests that
conceptual clarification should end in confession. If an unbelieving
philosopher at the end of the conference were to say "I have come
to see that the claims of Christianity are true," that would normally
be taken as a confession of faith. He might then utter, not a prayer
for understanding, but a prayer of thanksgiving: "Lord, Thou
knowest that I came to the conference too busy to think of Thee.
Yet, in Thy mercy, Thou didst remember me." If that happens, it
happens. There are times when it is difficult to distinguish between
philosophical and religious clarification. Yet distinctions can and
must be made between them. The second part of Hollis's remarks
suggest that he might recognize this, but I am not sure. He invites
us to consider the implications of taking away the quotation marks
from "religious knowledge." What this means, I suspect, is that
Hollis is inviting us to consider whether "religious knowledge" is
really knowledge, whether it satisfies some paradigm of knowledge. If this is so, some one use of "knowledge" is being elevated
above our diverse practices as a standard they must comply with. I
have said enough already to indicate why this would be another
example of subliming the logic of our language. Our question
should be, not whether we can remove the quotation marks from
"religious knowledge," but why we put them there in the first
place. Our conceptual task is to recognize the differences in our
uses of "knowledge" and "belief." Recognizing the differences,

where morality and religion are concerned, need not lead to the personal appropriation of what has been clarified.

As we have seen, Quinn says that in certain contexts he is resigned to epistemic relativism. He says "there is no realistic prospect that, in the foreseeable future, further applications of the techniques of critical rationalism [Jarvie's notion] will alter matters in the direction of convergence on a single consensus about rational or justified moral beliefs. Rational disagreement is highly likely to persist for a very long time over large areas of the landscape of the moral domain" ("Comments," p. 113). The example Quinn gives to illustrate the point, however, is of a clash between rival ethical theories in philosophy:

> Consider, for instance, the quarrel between the tradition of moral inquiry that favors a virtue ethics of Aristotelian or Thomistic provenance and the tradition that endorses a deontological ethics of a Kantian kind. Each tradition criticizes the other and responds to criticism by the other, but neither has been shown by the criticism of the other that it currently confronts problems which, by its own lights, it ought to be able to solve but lacks the resources to solve. The adherents of each tradition are within their epistemic rights in having the moral beliefs presently characteristic of that tradition; those beliefs are rational and fully justified. (Ibid., pp. 112f)

I may share, with Quinn, pessimism about the hope for change in the situation he describes, but for very different reasons. His regret consists in the fact that rival theories do not seem likely to reach a consensus. My regret concerns the persistence of such theories. There will always be counter-examples which *any* theory will be unable to accommodate. In their attempts to do so, the theories distort the counter-examples offered. The remedy is not to look for a theory which will accommodate any example offered, but to give up such theorizing. What we need to recognize is the reality of the moral differences.[9] If someone has moral beliefs which are accommodated within the traditions Quinn mentions, there is no philosophical objection to them. If that someone goes on to claim that any moral belief *must* take that form, then there is a philosophical objection to what they say. They have erected theories which deny space for other possibilities. These other possibilities are in our midst. They are the ordinary phenomena which need to be recognized, but our metaphysical dress gets in the way.

Yet, pessimistic though we may be about the outcome, there is no alternative to philosophical discussion. There is no short cut by which it can be bypassed. In the course of the present discussion, I have been accused of a revisionist program, of prescribing rather than describing. But it will not do to provide, as proof of this, long-standing modes of argument indulged in by philosophers of religion. The presence of such modes of argument is not disputed. But I say their presence is both confusing and distorting. And so discussion commences about that. In the course of it, considerations may be put to me which make me revise what I have said, and the same may happen to those with whom I disagree. My accusation, up for discussion, is that the metaphysical views of my opponents is a fancy dress which obscures the ordinary from us. At times my criticisms may hide the fact that I, too, am not immune from the attractiveness of that dress. I have to keep reminding myself that if I got all dressed up, I'd have nowhere to go.

I am sure that looking back at the conference and its deliberations, we can all join in a prayer for understanding. I fear, however, that what that prayer would come to in its details would again reveal differences between us. If we consider what I have been saying about metaphysical theories in the light of the following remark by Wittgenstein – "The solution of philosophical problems can be compared with a gift in a fairy tale: in the magic castle it appears enchanted and if you look at it outside in daylight it is nothing but an ordinary bit of iron (or something of the sort)" [*Culture and Value*, p. 11] – it is clear what the content of our prayer should be: "God grant the philosopher insight into what lies in front of everyone's eyes" (ibid., p. 63).

Notes

1. For eight examples of subliming the logic of our language in contemporary philosophy of religion, see my "Sublime Existence," *Archivio di Filosofia*, vol. LVIII, 1990, reprinted in *Wittgenstein and Religion* (London: Macmillan, 1992).
2. For a textual refutation of the theses of Wittgensteinian fideism see my *Belief, Change and Forms of Life* (London: Macmillan, 1986).
3. Simone Weil, *Lectures on Philosophy* (Cambridge: Cambridge University Press, 1978), p. 171.
4. The quotation is from an earlier version of Jarvie's essay (Ed.).

5. For detailed criticisms of Frazer, Tylor, Marett, Durkheim and Freud, see my *Religion Without Explanation* (Oxford: Blackwell, 1976).

6. For my criticism of a realist analysis of "believing," one which places it beyond all contexts of application, see "On Really Believing," "How Real is Realism?" and "Great Expectations" in *Is God Real?* ed. J. Runzo (London: Macmillan, 1992). The first of these papers is reprinted in *Wittgenstein and Religion*, op. cit. For a related criticism of attempts to give God's reality a sense independent of any linguistic context, see my "Searle on Language Games and Religion," *Tijdschrift voor Filosofie*, no. 2, 1989. This paper is also reprinted in *Wittgenstein and Religion*, op. cit.

7. For further criticisms of the notion, see *Belief, Change and Forms of Life*, op. cit.

8. Rush Rhees, "Reflections on Christian Doctrines," an unpublished paper from the Rush Rhees Archive. The title is mine.

9. This is a recurring theme in my essays in *Interventions in Ethics* (London: Macmillan, 1992).

Index